D0110640

"Everything there is to know about job interviewing can be found in *Winning Job Interviews*. There is nothing left out, there is nothing further that needs to be said or written. I recommend this book to CEOs, first-time job seekers, or individuals changing careers."

—Les B. Strauss, president/CFO, SuperWater Solutions, Inc.

"Dr. Paul Powers is the mentor we all wish we had when embarking on our first job search. He has assembled a wealth of practical advice on how to find a job and get hired, and delivers it in plain English sprinkled with his usual off-beat humor."

—Pat Hyland, executive director,
Northeast Public Power Association

"This new edition has lots of solid, easy-to-use information about the new technological tools that are essential for today's job hunters. A concise, practical, thorough guide to the job changing process that is filled with the warmth and humor to help you succeed."

—Stephen A. Bishop, PhD, president, Learning Services, Inc.

"This book will be useful for everyone from the recent graduate to the seasoned executive. If you are looking for the job that is right for you, this is the book to read. Powers prepares you for all facets of the job hunt from determining who is hiring in your area to closing the interview the right way."

—P. Scott Flagg, senior VP, Jeanne D'Arc Credit Union

"A clear, positive, and realistic guide for making magic, again and again, in your career."

—Cliff Hakim, career consultant and best-selling author of
We Are All Self-Employed

"Finally, an interview book that truly connects with the *person* who is going through the job-search process. Dr. Paul's practical and inspirational guidance turns anxieties into opportunities. Read it and tell all of your friends about this book."

—John Sullivan, director, sales training, Acushnet Company

"*Winning Job Interviews* provides insight, motivation, a strong dose of reality (and some well-needed humor) for professionals in today's tough job market. I wish every job candidate crossing my path would read and learn from this book."

—Scott S. Rassoulian, director of engineering,
Crane Aerospace Microelectronics

"Dr. Paul has written a great book filled with information that is paramount to acing the interview process. His solid advice and wry humor is a formula for success."

—Salvatore Calvino, president, Quantem Aviation Services, Inc.

WINNING

JOB

INTERVIEWS

Revised Edition

DR. PAUL POWERS

CAREER
PRESS

Franklin Lakes, N.J.

WINNING JOB INTERVIEWS, REVISED EDITION
EDITED AND TYPESET BY KARA KUMPEL
Cover design by Rob Johnson/Johnson Design
Printed in the U.S.A. by Courier

To order this title, please call toll-free 1-800-CAREER-1 (NJ and Canada: 201-848-0310) to order using VISA or MasterCard, or for further information on books from Career Press.

The Career Press, Inc., 3 Tice Road, PO Box 687, Franklin Lakes, NJ 07417
www.careerpress.com

Library of Congress Cataloging-in-Publication Data
Powers, Paul.
    Winning job interviews / by Paul Powers.--Rev. ed.
        p. cm.
    Includes index.
    ISBN 978-1-60163-088-9
    1. Employment interviewing. 2. Job hunting. I. Title.

HF5549.5.I6P69 2010
650.14'4—dc22
                                                            2009036390

For Dr. Norma Jean Anderson, former dean and professor emeritus, University of Massachusetts, Amherst, whose belief in a world of endless possibilities continues to be a source of motivation and inspiration.

For Dr. E.M. Beekman, Dr. O.C. Bobby Daniels, Dr. Edward Deevy, Dr. Ted Slovin, and Dr. Donald White: mentors, colleagues, and friends from the University of Massachusetts, Amherst, each of whom challenged me to question old assumptions and to trust the authority of my own experience.

For the unsung heroes who make any great university work, such as my friends at the University of Massachusetts who staff the Career Services, Veterans Services, Alumni Affairs, and Development offices.

ACKNOWLEDGMENTS

I would be remiss if I didn't acknowledge some folks whose support has been critical to this project. Ron Fry, Kirsten Beucler, Michael Pye, Adam Schwartz, Kristen Parkes, Kirsten Dalley, and everyone at Career Press helped bring this book to life in just the way I had hoped. Deborah Russell, my great pal and *Love Your Job!* coauthor, contributed improvements to *every* page. My wonderful wife, Linda Powers, makes all things possible with her unreserved support, sustaining confidence, and abundant love. A special thank-you goes to the readers of the first edition of *Winning Job Interviews* and the readers of my LifeMap newsletter (free subscription at *www.drpaulpowers.com*) for their stories, comments, and suggestions for this revised edition.

CONTENTS

INTRODUCTION

Winning Job Interviews is a book with attitude. The job-hunting process in general, and job interviewing in particular, require focus, energy, optimism, and a sense of humor. In the pages of this book you will find liberal doses of each. You won't find a lot of extraneous material to distract you from what you *really* need to know about job hunting and interviewing success. You *will* find a no-nonsense toolkit that will help you hit the ground running—if only you invest the energy required. I have poured my natural optimism and my years of hands-on professional experience onto every page, and they give me 100-percent confidence that you can become a winning job interviewer.

When I was in graduate school, back in the mid- to late 1970s, I had the wonderful opportunity to work with Vietnam-era veterans, similar to myself, on a host of issues that included career assessment, educational planning, and career counseling. With my new doctorate in hand, I joined the noted Dr. Alan Sostek in a management consulting practice that included the Career Center in downtown Boston. To get a more in-depth understanding of modern career development practices, I later became vice president of a well-known outplacement consulting firm and then joined a prestigious executive search firm.

Ultimately, 20 years ago, I established my own broad-based practice in management psychology, working with employees from the loading dock to the executive suite and in a vast array of industries—from hospitals to high-tech, from high-end financial services to not-for-profits, from gritty manufacturing floors to polished think-tank conference rooms. I have seen, inside and out, every element of the career process—recruiting new talent, selecting and training managers, coaching and counseling employees of all levels, relocating executives and their families, planning and implementing layoffs and RIFs (reductions in force), dealing with workplace violence, outplacement counseling, and pre-retirement planning.

In workshops and seminars, at conferences and conventions, in one-on-one counseling or coaching sessions, or just hanging out in the lunchroom (or now, huddled outdoors in the rain and wind with the smokers), untold numbers of people have honored me with the stories of their work lives—their hopes, their dreams, their fears, their failures. At the 30-year mark in my profession, I believe, now more fervently than ever before, that every individual must learn the skills to manage his or her own career and that you, truly, must be the captain of your own fate.

Perhaps you don't need a new job today. But remember: the economy is always taking either an upswing or a downturn. If you put to work what is in this short but powerful book you will be ready to either maximize your opportunities in a booming economy or to survive any recession and come out on top. That is what I call packing your own parachute, and, in either circumstance, you should start today.

Career management, job hunting, making a living, and job interviewing are all serious issues. Serious? Yes. Solemn? No. None of us get out of this life alive, my friend, and I've learned that a good laugh can help us endure and succeed in even the most difficult circumstances. (Or, as a friend of mine once said, "I might as well laugh at myself; everyone else is!") Thus, throughout this book, my little quips and humorous asides are meant to help you keep this whole process in its proper perspective. If you want a career book that will put you to sleep (and there are plenty of them out there), you'll have to look elsewhere. I'd never write a book I wouldn't read myself.

CHAPTER 1

WHY JOB HUNTING SUCKS (And What to Do About It)

This book is the shortest distance between you and a new job you can love. You—the motivated job hunter—can read it in one weekend or couple of nights and become one of the most skilled job hunters in any field, in any economic climate. But first you need to know what you are up against and how to deal with it.

If I were writing this book for other psychologists, career coaches, or outplacement experts, I would have called this chapter "Identifying and Resolving the Negative Psychosocial Consequences Perceived by Individuals in the Employment Transition Process." Not a bad title for a master's thesis or doctoral dissertation. But I'm writing this book for you, the job hunter, who needs solid input that is market-proven, quickly usable, and with no punches pulled—so let's call a spade a spade.

I don't need to convince you that job hunting sucks, because you already know it. If you don't know for sure, you probably have a strong sense that it does. And you wouldn't be too far from wrong. Although the job interview is the single most important element of the job-changing process, it is critical for you to remember that it is only one part—paramount though it may be—of an entire process. And for you to succeed, to win, in these critical interview situations, you must have a firm, realistic understanding of the whole job-hunting process. Armed with the knowledge in this book, you will be able to control the process, not be controlled by it; you will be able to drive the process rather than be driven crazy by it.

People who have recently completed the job-hunting process will tell you that it is one of the hardest things they have ever had to do. Sure, there is the occasional lucky person who has a new job fall in his lap—sports stars, former politicians, media figures. Good for them, but it has never happened to me, and I'll bet it has never happened to you. For the rest of us ordinary schnooks, job hunting is hard work. But now, finally, some good news: the hard work you invest in your job hunt will pay off in positive ways like almost nothing else.

The rewards for fully engaging yourself in this demanding job-hunting process are many: You can find a team of people with whom you enjoy working, you can find a boss you respect, you can add to your social circle, you can find colleagues or mentors from whom you can learn, you may actually make more money, and, best of all, you can discover work that has personal meaning for you beyond a mere paycheck. You will feel more professionally accomplished and more personally competent. You will have more energy and vitality that you can share with those closest to you, and, thus, you will receive more from them in return. You will be building a continuously reinforcing cycle of achievement and success in multiple areas of your life.

This all sounds terrific, but if this process can bring such wonderful rewards, why do the vast majority of job hunters hate it so much? The answer is that there is a predictable series of psychological stumbling blocks—I call them the **deadly dozen**—that can trip up even the most determined job hunter.

THE DEADLY DOZEN:
ROADBLOCKS OF JOB HUNTING

From more than 20 years of working in different areas of the career field, I have identified a dozen major psychological roadblocks that can sidetrack, confuse, and discourage even the most dedicated job hunter. These roadblocks are both powerful and insidious; they are at work even when you can't see them. They are among the strongest reasons that many people stay in dead-end jobs or try to avoid the job-hunting process at all costs—to the detriment of their careers and the overall quality of their lives.

If you are going to be a successful job hunter (and this, in no small part, means becoming a winning job interviewee), you will need to recognize, face up to, and overcome each of these factors. By getting these roadblocks out in the open and learning how to get around them, you will automatically put yourself in the top tier of smart job hunters. With my help you can do it, so let's get started.

Roadblock #1:
Lack of a Crisp, Clear, Realistic Goal

Some job hunters start the process by making a few phone calls looking for leads or scanning the help-wanted ads in their local newspaper for "something interesting" or "a place where I can use my people skills." When this initial effort fails (as it often does) to turn up something wonderful in a relatively short period of time, the typical job hunter starts to get discouraged. You hear them say, "We're in a bad job market these days," or, "There's nothing much available in my field right now," or, "This isn't a good time of the year to be looking," and so on.

She then begins to put in even less effort, and, predictably, gets even fewer, if any, positive results. Soon this becomes a self-reinforcing cycle of defeat. It overwhelms the job hunter and convinces her that maybe she'd better just hang onto the mediocre job she has now or settle for something that's easy to find or that may be beneath what she's capable of. This is Roadblock #1 at its worst.

Although it's not very politically correct to talk about it much these days, I want you to think for a moment about an actual hunter. One who is out in the woods. If it makes you feel more comfortable, set him back in time before food for the family table was found shrink-wrapped in plastic, injected with preservatives, and stacked like cordwood in your local Mega-Mart. If this hunter wants his family to eat tonight, he has to know exactly what he's hunting for, he has to be able to recognize it when he sees it, he will need to have a detailed knowledge of the terrain, and he will have practiced his hunting skills until they are nearly flawless. Otherwise his family goes hungry. It is easy to see the clear parallels here to the job-hunting process.

The first step in any successful job search is to develop a clear, crisp, realistic goal. If you can't describe what job you are looking for in one or two sentences, then you are not ready to be out there in the job market asking for interviews.

You must be ready to clearly state what type of position you are looking for, in what type of organization, and in what geographic area, and you must be able to make a persuasive case based upon your knowledge, your experience, and your personal characteristics as to why someone should hire you to do this job for a reasonable salary. If you are not armed with this information, you are going to waste a lot of time and energy spinning your wheels, getting lost, and pursuing targets that are inappropriate or not worth your effort.

You must overcome this roadblock before you attempt to move your job search into high gear. If you know exactly what you're looking for, where to look for it, and how best to find it—great! But if you are not sure you're fully ready to conduct a professional, fine-tuned, multi-front job campaign, turn to Chapter 9, which is the Winning Job Interview Toolkit, and get to work on Tool #1: Am I Ready to Job Hunt?

Roadblock #2:
No Control Over the Timing of the Job Hunt

Job hunting is such an unpleasant task that most folks wait until something beyond their control forces them to make a move. Maybe it's an RIF, a layoff, a plant closing, a merger, a product recall, a boss bringing in his own team, or jobs being sent overseas that provides the motivation. Maybe you saw the writing on the wall but didn't have time to jump instead of being pushed. If this hasn't yet happened to you in your career, stay tuned, because one day it surely will. The reality is that very few of us take the bull by the horns and get an aggressive, professional job search underway before we are told that we have to.

Despite the initial discomfort that comes with any one of these scenarios, it's actually one of those "good news/bad news" things. The bad news is obvious. The vast majority of job hunters are thrown into a process that makes great demands on them for energy, creativity, and productivity—all while playing *Beat the Clock* with their income, severance pay or unemployment compensation, and (God willing) savings on the one hand, and their outgoing cash flow and bills on the other. It's no small wonder that many job hunters get down in the dumps.

If you are resentful that you have to job hunt at a time not of your own choosing, you must address this issue and get it out of the way. Seek your employee assistance program, outplacement consultant, or career or unemployment counselor for advice. Locate and join a job-search networking/support group. If you are finding it impossible to concentrate on your job hunt because you are constantly obsessing or worried about money, sharpen your pencil and work out a realistic budget for a job hunt with a realistic time line.

Don't try to ignore this feeling, because it will surface when you want it least. Some anxiety is normal and predictable in any job search. But if it escalates into panic, it can affect your behavior as well as your attitude. You may expect things to happen too quickly, and not reaching these unrealistic goals will create more anxiety. It will push you to look and sound desperate, and this attitude is the death of winning job interviews. It will impair your vision so that you may see the first job that pops up, perhaps one that's only so-so, as a good job that you should take.

You're probably asking, "Okay, Paul, so what's the *good* news already?" Well, the good news is that you are completely free to actively and professionally pursue the job of your dreams on a full-time basis. You are not limited to job hunting on your lunch hour or when the boss isn't around. You no longer have to sneak off to interviews during phony dentist appointments. You don't have to worry about having someone overhear you on the phone or look over your shoulder while you're on your computer. You can freely ask your current colleagues for their input, advice, and networking contacts. You can ask your human resources person for referrals to employment agencies. All of these actions will help you succeed in your job hunt—more quickly than if you had to do it on an on-the-sly, part-time basis.

In no way am I suggesting that you ignore the fact that your financial situation may be somewhat precarious and demand more thought, a tighter budget, or perhaps some alternative arrangements (that is, temping, part-time work, consulting, and so on). I merely want to reinforce for you that thousands and thousands of job hunters have somehow scraped by financially *and* found great jobs at a time not of their choosing. You can too.

Roadblock #3: Nobody Likes Being a Rookie

One of the hardest days at any job is your first day. Even if it is very similar to a job you have held previously, you still have to find out how this organization does things and who the right people are to ask for help, and you have to learn all the ins and outs of the informal organization. It's no fun being the rookie. It's like being the new kid at school.

When you are suddenly back in the job market, you are beginning a difficult and demanding task that you may not have done many times before, and maybe you didn't even do so well at it last time. Let's face it: we all like to do things either that we are good at or that we enjoy. Although we will be called upon many more times than our parents ever were during their careers to go out job hunting, most of us will never do it enough to get very good at it. And even fewer of us will ever learn to enjoy the process.

Maybe you didn't keep good notes or records during your last job hunt so you're feeling as if you're starting from scratch. (This won't happen to you again because Tool #16 in the Toolkit is the Job Search Wrap-Up Tool.) Maybe you realize that job interviewing is a skill that improves dramatically with practice—and realize you're out of practice.

One of the unrealistic expectations of job hunting is that most people feel they must excel in a process at which they are not very good, and if they don't succeed fairly quickly, they believe their lives will be screwed up. If you feel this way, you need some realistic data from the job-hunting world. Through your network contacts, unemployment office, or outplacement counselor, find a couple of other job hunters who are further along in their job hunt than you are in yours. Ask how they got up to speed with their job search. Be sure to pick positive-thinking, motivated people to help you overcome this common roadblock.

Roadblock #4: It's All About Rejection

Few people in life thrive on rejection. Salespeople have learned how to do this, and the most successful salespeople I've ever met seem to be built in a different way psychologically from the rest of us. Saying no to a good salesperson is not like saying no to the rest of us. To them, a no means *not yet* or *you haven't told me enough* or *maybe later* or *we need to negotiate about price or timing or something else*. A successful salesperson doesn't take the first, second, or even third no as a bona fide rejection. (By the way, this is one of the reasons salespeople make such effective job hunters.)

But how many of the rest of us really thrive on rejection? I don't—do you? The job-hunting process is nothing but a series of rejections with an occasional piece of good news thrown in just to keep you from sticking your head in the oven. Let's think about this for a minute.

The typical job hunt goes like this: Time after time you go through the process of uncovering a job lead through whatever method you used that day, chasing this lead with a resume, following up with a letter and a series of phone calls, working your way through a series of interviews, sending out the thank-you letters, getting your hopes up—and all for the net result of probably not getting the job. Sounds fun, eh?

Being realistic, you will probably go through this process a number of times before the job you really want comes through. Another unfortunate reality—but a reality that must be faced nonetheless—is that the job-hunting process contains a whole lot more rejection than acceptance.

The biggest key to overcoming this roadblock is understanding that this is the essential nature of the process. Getting rejected doesn't mean you're doing it wrong; it means you're doing it right! In fact, I tell job hunters that if they aren't getting rejected a lot, then either they aren't job hunting hard enough or they aren't searching for a job that represents a step up for them.

Another way to overcome this sense of rejection is to realize that the employer didn't make a decision *not to hire* you. They made a decision *to hire* somebody else. Obviously, that person made a better case or looked to be a better fit than you did. Try to come up with some ideas as to how you could have presented yourself in a stronger light and try those techniques during your next interview. Put this hard-won information to work for you by including it in your post-interview notes. (To help you do this, use Tool #13, the Post-Interview Evaluation and Improvement Tool, in the Toolkit.) Remember: this is a learning process. You'll get better at it in time.

Finally, don't be paranoid. No one has so little to do or so much time on their hands that they are out there interviewing people just to be able to sadistically reject them. It may feel that way, but it ain't true.

Roadblock #5: It's Unpredictable

By and large, human beings don't like surprises. I know that I don't. Okay, maybe I like that rare piece of unexpected good news or a letter from a friend or a thoughtful thank-you. But I'm willing to bet that people in funny hats jumping out of dark closets are responsible for more heart attacks than expressions of unbridled delight. When the doorbell rings late at night, I'm under no illusion that it's the Publisher's Clearing House Prize Patrol!

This, most likely, goes back to our caveman past when a big, exciting surprise was apt to be something like an 800-pound, snarling, saber-toothed tiger about to rip the head from our shoulders. Surprises were usually bad news. (Think about this the next time you're crouching in the dark in somebody's front hall closet with their raincoats and umbrellas.) To heck with surprises, give me predictability.

Well, guess what? The job-hunting process is totally unpredictable except for one thing: If you work hard at it, you *will* eventually get a job. And this one certainty is something that you will have to take from me on faith. And, although you may believe this intellectually, there will be discouraging days during your job hunt when it will *feel* as if you'll never get a job.

Let's take a look at all the uncertainties of the job search: You don't know how long your job search will take. You don't know the name of the organization in which you will end up working. You don't know the specific job you will end up doing. You don't know who will be your boss. You don't know where this organization will be located. You don't know who your peers will be. You may not know the industry your employer will be in. You don't know the details of your salary and benefits. With all these uncertainties, it is only natural to be apprehensive about the job-hunting process.

One caller to my *CareerTalk* radio show said it best: "Being a job hunter is worse than being a convict in prison. A convict at least knows when he is eligible for parole so he can make some plans for the future. But a job hunter is more like a hostage, because there is no set date to pin one's hopes on. You just have to tough it out day by day and keep the faith that something good will eventually happen." This is a pretty stark analogy, but there is wisdom in it. If you work hard at your search and you keep the faith that something good will happen, it will. I just can't predict when. Sorry 'bout that.

Roadblock #6: It Lacks Structure

In my previous book, *Love Your Job!*, I identify many of the benefits of having a great job. Heck, one of the benefits of even a so-so job is that it provides structure to your everyday life.

For most of us, structure is comfortable; it's knowing what time to get up in the morning, knowing the route or method of your commute, knowing who you will be working with, having a basic understanding of the types of challenges you will face during the day, knowing (perhaps praying for) the time you will be done for the day, and knowing what time you need to go to bed to get enough rest to do it all over again tomorrow.

The job hunt, for the unemployed person especially, does not provide this kind of structure. The amount of time you spend on any particular job-hunting technique is up to you. The sequence in which you tackle tasks is up to you. The amount of energy and drive you put into your search is up to you. The time of day you start and the time of day you stop working is up to you. Who you will see and who you will not see is up to you. You are now running a completely independent operation.

To some folks, this independence is exhilarating. It's like running your own business just as you've always dreamed. To others, it feels like being cut adrift, alone in a small boat, with no idea which direction to row in order to get home. If you thrive on this degree of self-direction, you are fortunate. If you don't, don't beat yourself up about it. The majority of the world feels the same way you do. Here's how you deal with it.

If you found yourself on a desert island with nothing to protect you from the wind and rain, what would you do? Think back to Tom Hanks in the movie *Castaway*. Obviously, you would build a shelter. It might not be perfect at first, but in time you would improve this structure, making it stronger, more secure, and more comfortable. You wouldn't build more structure than you needed. Nor would you build one that wouldn't meet your needs. This is what you must do during your job search: build a structure that meets your needs.

You must force yourself to answer such questions as these: What time will I start on my job search each morning? What are my weekly goals? What are my monthly goals? When do I predict I will be reemployed? When will I go to the library to do my research? How much time will I devote to networking? How many sources of published openings will I review weekly? How many employment agency/search firm contacts are enough? How much time should I spend on the telephone? You must recognize that you are now self-employed, and the only person who can answer these questions is you.

The only structure you will find in the job-hunting process is the one you provide for yourself. If you need it, it only makes sense to build it for yourself and come in out of the rain. (Tool #3 in the Toolkit, Job Hunt Goal-Setting and Monitoring, will help you set, customize, and reach your weekly and monthly job search goals.)

Roadblock #7: It Requires Asking for Help

Both men and women stumble over this roadblock, though I have observed a much higher percentage of men struggling with this one. Let's use an example to which most of us can relate. Have you ever noticed a person continually driving around and around the same block, craning his neck looking for street numbers or landmarks, and swerving from one side of the road to the other while frantically glancing down at a scrap of paper held in one hand? What's going on here?

You guessed it. He's lost. Now, whereas some of us would prefer to use such terms as "momentarily disoriented," "geographically impaired," or "temporarily uncertain as to *exact* position," this guy needs help. Why is it that some people would rather struggle along with a problem by themselves than to ask for help from others?

Some have suggested that men have this problem because of sex-role stereotyping, as in, "I'm a manly man. I don't *need* help, I *give* help!" This is probably true to some extent, but it doesn't explain why some women also labor needlessly in this regard. Perhaps it has less to do with gender (nature) and more to do with the degree of independence we were accustomed to in our environment as we grew up (nurture). Whatever the reason, it is counterproductive to your job-hunting success, and it will make the process both longer and more difficult.

If you have an "I must do it on my own" attitude, you've got to overcome it. To help you do this, I have compiled **Dr. Paul's Short Course on Humility**. To complete this course, read the statements on the following page and respond with True or False.

I know exactly what types of jobs are available in my geographical area and occupational field.	True	False
I know precisely the salary ranges and benefits these jobs provide.	True	False
I know every source of print and on-line job postings/help-wanted ads for people in my field.	True	False
I know of and can speak to all employment agencies and search firms that work in my field.	True	False
I am confident that my resume and my letters are the best they can be.	True	False
I am completely familiar with all the Websites, blogs, libraries, schools, colleges, and public offices that have relevant information I will need during my job search.	True	False
Secretaries and administrative assistants swoon at the mere sound of my voice and always put my phone calls through on my first try.	True	False
I have a personal network of between 100 and 200 people who will be willing to help me with my job search. And I know how to get them to help me.	True	False
I love making telephone calls to people I don't know.	True	False
When faced with rejection, I never get discouraged.	True	False
When faced with a difficult, frustrating task, I find that isolation and lack of brainstorming help me to become more creative.	True	False

If you answered false to *any* of these items, you need help. This is not a weakness; it is part and parcel of the job-hunting game. Whenever you are tempted to tough it out alone, remember Dr. Paul's Short Course on Humility. Humility means putting your pride in your pocket. And by doing that, I guarantee, a paycheck will soon follow.

Roadblock #8:
It Requires Blowing One's Own Horn

If it seems as if I've been picking on men, the tables are about to turn. Another reason job hunting seems so difficult is that you have to "blow your own horn." Many people (and here I find a much higher percentage are women) have a hard time selling themselves. Many of us were taught that it is not polite or seemly to talk about ourselves, all the wonderful things we have accomplished or the kudos we've received, or all the insightful thoughts we have or the many terrific personal characteristics we have developed.

One frustrated job hunter once said to me, "I hate this. I'm a back-office type. If I wanted to be a salesperson, I would have *become* one." My response was, "You are a job hunter, which means you've just been transferred to the sales department. Welcome aboard!" (With his funky mood, I was lucky he didn't strangle me.)

To overcome this hesitancy to sell yourself, you will need practice, coaching, and feedback. By the way, this is how average salespeople become great salespeople. When you talk to a close contact about your job search, ask if you came on too strong or if it would be better to come on a little stronger. When you meet recruiters, ask them for feedback about your personal presentation. If you discover important accomplishments that you've neglected to put on your resume, be sure to revise it to include them. If after some of your preliminary interviews you feel comfortable with an interviewer, ask him for some feedback about your style.

No prospective employer looks at the hiring process as a detective job or a hidden treasure hunt. They will learn only as much about you as you are willing to share. The more data you put on the table about yourself, as it relates to this employment opportunity, the better chance you stand of getting the job offer you want. It's that simple. If you sit there waiting and hoping to be discovered, like a starlet in some 1940s movie, you will fail.

Roadblock #9: It's Lonely and Isolating

To the unemployed job hunter, it looks as though everybody else in the entire world has a job. People driving down your street during the morning commute seem clearly different from you. They have someplace they *have to* be, where there are people with whom they *have to* meet. You, on the other hand, are on your own to figure out for yourself what it is that you have to do. During off hours, many job hunters feel that their friends and family don't want to hear about their job search because, somehow, it reflects negatively on them that they are unemployed. And, after all, who wants to be continually giving the bad news: "No, I haven't found a job yet."

If you are gainfully employed while looking for a job, it can be even lonelier because, realistically, there are very few people at work with whom you should risk discussing your job search. I have observed that the *best* bosses, those interested in their employees' growth and career development, are quite willing to have their employees know what their career options are in the open job market. However, not all bosses are that secure, and most folks have good reason to fear that their boss will hear through the grapevine (as Marvin Gaye would say) that they are actively looking for a new job.

These and other factors combine to make the job-hunting process a lonely and isolating experience. The problem is that loneliness and isolation are the mortal enemies of high energy and a positive attitude, both of which you will need in order to succeed as a job hunter. The way to overcome this roadblock is to learn that you cannot succeed at this process by yourself; you will need other people.

If you are looking for a job while unemployed, there are a number of ways to connect with other job hunters who can keep you from becoming lonely and isolated. If you have outplacement assistance, be sure to avail yourself of the group meetings and networking forums the outplacement firm provides. Most state unemployment or employment and training offices offer networking support groups. Many community and church groups now either sponsor job-search networking groups or let such groups use their facilities. For example, in Massachusetts alone, I have a list of 36 such groups. Get involved in these groups and you will be amazed at how useful they will be to help you generate leads, keep focused, and keep you connected with other people.

If you are looking for a job while employed and don't want to join a public networking group, you will have to construct one of your own. By talking with your associates at work, your friends, your family, and a large range of contacts, you can probably identify four to six people who are looking for a new job at any one time. Try to organize regular group meetings. Or, if that is impossible, try discussing your job search with each one individually and encourage them to discuss their job search with you. Reinforce the confidential nature of these conversations. Ask each of them if they know one or two other current job hunters you could include in a private and confidential job-search networking group. Take it upon yourself to organize this group. Set up a regular meeting time and organize an agenda. Attend the meeting of a public group to see how it's done.

So that you have both sides of the story, yes, I have seen a few folks who toughed out a job search almost entirely on their own. And yes, they all ultimately landed jobs. But it was harder, it took longer, and it was tougher on them and those around them than it had to be. Finding (or building) and using a networking support group is easier, quicker, less stressful, and more fun. What's not to like?

Roadblock #10: Self-Doubt, Defensiveness, and the Myth of the Perfect Job Candidate

Every human being has a weak spot. It may be real or imagined; it may be in your education, your work history, your appearance, your skills, or your background. Maybe you are aware of your weak spot, and maybe you aren't.

If you are in the dark about your weak spot, here's a quick way to uncover it. Complete the following sentence: *It would be a lot easier for me to get a job if only I...*

This is your job-hunting weak spot. (This is a good exercise to do every so often during your job hunt.) When someone else raises the issue that you already believe to be a weak spot, it is only natural for you to defend yourself. But—and you've seen this in others—defensiveness negatively affects the sound of your voice, closes up your body language, stunts your creativity, makes you less open in your responses, and generally makes you a less attractive person. These are the exact opposites of the things that you want happening to you during your job search, and especially during your interviews.

The way to overcome job-search defensiveness is to do a fair and honest self-assessment. You have to gain a balanced understanding of your relative strengths and weaknesses, and learn how to best present them to potential employers. Perhaps you have a career counselor, outplacement consultant, employment specialist, or organizational psychologist who can help you with this. You can find many helpful self-assessment exercises in my earlier book, *Love Your Job! Loving the Job You Have, Finding a Job You Love* (O'Reilly Media, 1993). A supportive friend or colleague can help you with this. But, whatever you do, you will need to have as clear and objective a picture of who you are and what it is that you have to offer a hiring organization as possible. If you do not do this, you will have planted a booby trap for yourself that will go off when you least want it to during your job search.

What is it that determines who is hired for any particular job? Is it qualifications alone? No. Is it education alone? No. Is it work experience alone? No. Is it personality alone? No. Is it references alone? No. Is it a great resume alone? No. Is it contacts alone? No. Is it luck alone? No. Is it that you bought the right book? As much as I want to say yes, the answer is no! What determines if you are hired for a specific job is (a) a combination of all of these factors, plus (b) your ability to communicate these factors.

Even though you may have a great education, strong resume, super background, extensive work experience, and terrific personal characteristics, there actually may be someone applying for the same job as you that is *stronger* than you are in one of these categories. Does this mean that person will certainly be hired and you will not? No. The reason for this is that the other candidate is probably not as strong as you are in some other category. Every job candidate represents a unique mix of background, skills, education, knowledge, and personality—a specific equation of strengths and weaknesses.

Unfortunately, many job hunters labor under what I call *the myth of the perfect job candidate.* This myth is based on the fear that some god-like figure who is terrific in every way is applying for the same job you are. It further suggests that because you are *not* terrific in every way, the interviewer will discover you for the imperfect, mere mortal that you are, and thus you will not get the job.

The way to overcome this self-doubt is to realize that there aren't many (if any) perfect job candidates out there, and we don't live in a perfect meritocracy anyway. It is a fact that the best person for a job doesn't necessarily get hired. There will be times when this reality will work for you and there will be times when it will work against you. But that doesn't change the reality. What can help in this regard is for you to memorize **Dr. Paul's #1 Rule of Successful Job Hunting**: *The most effective job hunter will get the most interviews, and the most effective interviewee will get the most and best job offers.*

Look, it's no secret to those who love you most in this world that you are nowhere close to perfect. But they still love you, right? So take a good look at your supposed weak spots, and with your hard work, sense of humor, and determination to succeed, I can help you to become an effective job hunter, a terrific interviewee, and a winning job candidate.

Roadblock #11: Your Baggage

What I call *your baggage* is an assortment of the unresolved, negative emotions you have collected during your life. They can originate from any area of your life: your family, your personal life, your education and training, or your work. They may have been communicated to you by parents, teachers, friends, enemies, spouses, bosses, peers, idiots, or geniuses.

Deep within each of us there is a place where we store good memories and bad, remembrances of achievements and failures, and hopes and fears for the future. Attached to each of these are emotions. When positive emotions (for example, love, happiness, acceptance, peaceful-ness, forgiveness) are touched upon by something happening in our daily lives, we are affected in both conscious and subconscious ways. Similarly, when negative emotions (for example, fear, jealousy, dread, anger, resentment) are stirred up, we also respond in conscious and subconscious ways. Although misplaced love can have a negative effect and righteous anger can have a positive effect, we can generally say that positive emotions have a positive effect and that negative emotions have a negative effect on our daily lives. This is especially true during the job-hunting process.

If you feel that you are job hunting because you were unjustly fired from your last job, the anger you feel toward your former boss may display itself in various ways during the job search. If you are envious or jealous of the position held by your interviewer, you may communi-cate this in your responses, your attitude, or your body language. If you are stalled by the fear of rejection or the fear of failure during your job change, you will take fewer risks, and, ultimately, you may accept a job that is beneath your aspirations.

Take a good, hard look at yourself and your attitudes about job hunting. Talk them over with a close friend, confidant, mentor, or counselor. What negative emotions about this process are you carrying around? Where did they come from? What are they based upon? Can you see where they might hurt you? What can you do about it? Some-times just talking these issues through can help you to put them aside. If that is not the case, try to come up with some competing positive emotions to pair them with to dampen their negative effect. Try to take a healthful, forgiving, and humorous look at the situations that spawned these situations.

If these ideas do not work for you, try using the exercises for positive thinking and realistic optimism in *Love Your Job!* The baggage I refer to weighs you down, trips you up, siphons off your energy, and may prevent you from reaching your full potential. The job hunt can be a rugged and bumpy stretch on your personal road to success. But if you dump some of that extra baggage you've been dragging along with you, you can lighten your load, relax a little, and, I hope, maybe even enjoy the ride a bit.

Roadblock #12:
The Psychology of Entitlement

A couple of years ago, a client company asked me to do some career coaching with one of their star managers. With a BS cum laude in psychology, Marilyn had gone into consumer sales with a prestigious consumer products company right out of college. After three and a half years, she was accepted into the Wharton School of Management. After receiving her MBA she was recruited into a well-known and widely respected mutual fund company in Boston as a marketing manager. Marilyn did well with this company, but after almost five years, the company was going to relocate her department to the Midwest, and they wanted her to go with it.

This relocation was something that Marilyn didn't want to do and felt she didn't need to do. When she wasn't offered a comparable position within the company, she informed her boss that she would rather resign than move. Her manager asked me to talk to her, because he wanted her to either (a) change her mind and relocate, or (b) if she did resign, to avail herself of the outplacement assistance that had been offered her, to which she had responded with something like a cross between disbelief and disdain.

I failed on both counts. (*Hmm, maybe I should be telling one of my success stories.*) Marilyn was dead set against relocating. Her view of the world was similar to that of the famous *New Yorker* magazine cover with Boston and New York on the far right, a frozen, nameless tundra on the top, California on the far left, and nothing in the middle.

Her attitude about outplacement was just as parochial and short-sighted: it was for losers, not high-flying winners such as herself. Marilyn's attitude was that with her educational credentials and her strong track record with great companies, she wouldn't need much help because people would be knocking down her door looking for someone with her profile and background.

The next time I saw Marilyn was when she came up to speak to me after I had given a pro bono speech to a local networking/support group for the unemployed—*five months* after I had last seen her! Five months isn't a particularly long job search for some jobs in some job

markets, but it had seemed like a geological era to Marilyn. She had
sent out a few resumes, contacted a couple of headhunters, and then sat
back to wait for the flood of wonderful offers. She was devastated that
she received only a couple of courtesy phone calls in response. (I told
her that, with the miniscule amount of effort expended on her part, I
was surprised that she received as much response as she had.) This
networking meeting was the first active step she had taken in weeks,
and that was only because a close friend had led her by the hand.

The moral of this story could be about willingness to relocate or
about utilizing whatever assistance one is offered, or even about humility, but it is not. The moral is that no matter what type of superior
background you feel you have, no matter what credentials you've earned,
no matter what prestigious educational pedigree you hold, no matter
how wonderful some people say you are, no one is going to come
knocking on your door with a basketful of wonderful and exciting
career opportunities just because you feel that you are entitled to them.
The psychology of entitlement—whether in your career, your family,
or your community—is a roadblock to your success and satisfaction in
any area of your life.

If you feel entitled to have your company, your former employer,
your outplacement firm, some employment agency, a search firm, your
network, or anyone or any other organization go out and find you
another job, I can guarantee that you will be spending a lot of time
home alone watching daytime television.

Sure, job hunting sucks. But nobody else will do it for you. Nobody *can* do it for you. Nobody *should* do it for you. Heck, there isn't
even anybody you can *pay* to do it for you.

In today's world of work there are no guarantees and there are no
entitlements. To achieve, you must push yourself to perform. To grow,
you must push yourself to learn. To advance, you must accept and
adapt to change. The responsibility for driving and advancing your
career is now, more than ever before, in your own hands. And that is
as it should be.

We've taken a hard look at the ways many people stumble during the job-hunting process. By examining the deadly dozen roadblocks to effective job hunting, I trust you now see that each of them can be overcome with knowledge, spirit, energy, humor, and optimism. That's our theme in *Winning Job Interviews*, so now let's move on to the mechanics of the process in the next chapter, "How to Get More and Better Interviews."

CHAPTER 2

HOW TO GET MORE AND BETTER INTERVIEWS

In Chapter 1 you learned Dr. Paul's #1 Rule of Successful Job Hunting: *The most effective job hunter will get the most interviews, and the most effective interviewee will get the most and the best job offers.* In Chapter 2 we are going to focus on making you one of the most effective job hunters, and we're going to do it as quickly as possible.

An effective job hunter is someone who is out there in the marketplace actively looking for a new opportunity—with knowledge, with energy, and with focus. When I'm at a party or gathering and people hear what I do for work and what I write about, I often get comments such as, "I'd like a better job," or, "I'm keeping my eyes open," or, "I'll take a look if something interesting comes along." With my wife's help, I've learned to button my yap, smile, and nod supportively (while looking for a refill). Prior to the civilizing effect that Linda has had on me, I used to get on my high horse and try to motivate these folks with the facts of job-hunting life. These people aren't job hunters; they're more like relaxed weekend bird-watchers. Maybe something will come along; maybe it won't. They are passively waiting and hoping for a more satisfying career. Don't get me wrong—patience and hope are great virtues, but winning in the job-hunting game takes drive, savvy, and a willingness to take risks.

REALISTIC, MARKET-TUNED

GOAL-SETTING

If you were planning a vacation or a major trip, how would you go about it? Most likely you would do a number of things before you ever made reservations to spend your hard-earned money. You would research the area you wanted to visit. You would make a list of the things you most enjoy doing, and then you'd find out if your destination offers them. You would find out what stuff costs. You would take inventory of what you have and make a list of what you need. You would ask family, friends, neighbors, and contacts for their ideas and input. In short, you would put together an informed plan of how to accomplish what you want to do on your vacation.

Embarking on an effective job hunt requires exactly this kind of thinking and planning. Before you ever step out into the job market, I want you to know the lay of the land. Certainly, you will learn a lot more than what immediately meets the eye as your job hunt progresses, but, even starting out, I want you to know more than your competition. To get your job hunt up and running as quickly and efficiently as possible, you need to know the following things right off the bat:

1. Who are the potential employers in my target geographical area?
2. Of these employers, which ones employ people with my skills, in my functional area?
3. Where can I learn about their history, products, and services?
4. Where do these employers advertise for help?
5. What employment agencies and recruiters do they use?
6. What online job listing or Web recruiting services do they use?
7. What is the typical pay or salary range for people with my skills in these types of organizations?

Perhaps you are a skilled and creative researcher and already have some ideas about where to find this essential job-hunting information.

If so, great. But for most of us, just the word *research* brings back memories of all the dull school projects we once struggled with. Regardless of how skilled you are as a researcher or how you feel about tracking down hard-to-find information, I have great news for you! You have, at your disposal, a knowledgeable and willing partner who will advise and consult with you in the research process. Oh, and I forgot to mention: this help won't cost you a penny.

Your New Best Friend

Your new best friend works downtown or maybe downtown in the next town over or maybe at the local college. She is a reference librarian. By nature these people like to know where information can be found, and by professional training they know how to find it. If you haven't visited the reference department of your local library lately, it's time to get your butt in there.

What you will find are hundreds and sometimes thousands of resources you can use in your job hunt: books about job hunting and interviewing, directories of employers, research guides to various industries, annual reports of companies you might want to work for, access to online databases for research, and Websites with job listings. It is a veritable treasure trove of valuable job-hunting information. Most libraries are members of library networks, and if you can't find something in your own library, the reference librarian can help you find stuff from all over the country.

But (you knew there had to be a *but*, didn't you?) your reference librarian is not your personal researcher. She is not there to wait on you hand and foot. You are not the only person who needs research help. She is there to teach you, to advise you, and to consult with you about how you can find the information you need. Be satisfied with this valuable and unexpected source of help, and learn how to dig out the information that will help you land a job you love.

When you first decide you are going to go job hunting, review the seven questions listed on page 38. With whatever resources you have already at hand, list all the relevant information you can. Then, when you have already begun the research process, go introduce yourself to the reference department at your local library. If your local library is not too great, try one in a neighboring town or at a local college. I want you to have started the process before you even go to the library for two reasons.

1. I want you to see how difficult it can be to find out what you need to know.

2. I want you to show your reference librarian that you have started on your own, that you know what you're looking for, that you realize her professional assistance is of great value to you, and that you are a willing student and will not be a drain on her time and patience. Alienating your local reference librarian is one of the worst things you can do when you're job hunting (or writing a book, or just trying to live an informed life).

When you first introduce yourself to the reference librarian, start by asking what resources are on hand that other job hunters have found most useful. I know the job hunt can be an isolating process, but you are not out there alone, nor are you the first person who has stumbled into the library looking for help. The librarian will ask you what type of job you are looking for and what types of organizations you're looking to find out about. This is why it is essential for you to have thought this stuff through before you go in looking for help. The more informed you get on your own, the more help the librarian can be. Oh, and librarians like people who are willing to work at it. But remember our *but*. They are not there to do the research for you. They are there to guide you, to advise you, and to help you do it on your own. Be thankful.

With this research process well underway, you now should have enough preliminary information to identify your initial job-hunting goals. You are already miles ahead of your competition, most of whom are working from inaccurate assumptions about the job market, rumors about who is hiring, and faulty or out-of-date job-hunting techniques. Your goals are realistic and market-tuned because they are based on current, accurate, and objective data. Congratulations—you're off to a great start.

HOW TO EFFECTIVELY IDENTIFY
YOUR JOB TARGETS

You now have your preliminary goals firmly in mind: you are looking for this type of job, in this type of organization; they typically find people through these avenues; and they typically pay people with your skills about this much money. What you need now are specific job targets.

There are dozens of different ways you can identify bona fide job targets, but, generally speaking, they all fit into one of four major job-hunting methods. These four methods, which I call the *four-front job campaign*, are: published openings, targeted mailings, recruiters, and networking. (Of course, there's always marrying for money or winning the lottery, but those are topics for other books.)

Traditional Sources: Published Openings

Help-Wanted Ads

Most people are familiar with this job-hunting method: the help-wanted ads. Some appear in your local paper, some in the local business press, and others in the major metropolitan papers. There are places other than the newspaper to look for published openings. Some are in technical journals, professional newsletters, union job banks, and state unemployment office listings.

Job Fairs

These are good opportunities to locate published openings in organizations that are hiring. If you can make a personal contact, then ask for a business card, see if there are any appropriate openings, leave a resume, and follow up later. But if a table or booth is mobbed, I suggest that you do not just throw your resume onto a pile, hoping it will come to someone's notice later on. Try to get a business card from whomever is representing the company (usually a rep from human resources). Later you can follow up by e-mail or phone stating that you were in attendance, and unable to get through the crush of people, but would like to uncover any openings that might be a fit for your background.

Online Resources/Job Boards

We've all heard of the big job boards thanks to the Super Bowl half-time ads. There are tens of thousands of career-related sites, so even the best researcher will need a strategy. Here's the three-step process I suggest:

Step 1. Start with the clearinghouses. They collect tons of useful job-hunting and career info and are a great place to start. My favorites: quintcareers.com, job-hunt.org, and careerjournal.com.

Step 2. Move on to the big job boards. They are the supersites with millions of job positions. They can be tiring, and searching can be tedious, but using them can be facilitated by becoming familiar with the search criteria specific to each site. My favorites: Monster.com, CareerBuilder.com, and HotJobs.Yahoo.com. You can also try a couple of aggregator sites. They search for appropriate openings on multiple job sites. My favorites: jobster.com, simplyhired.com, and indeed.com.

Step 3. Find sites that focus on your specific function, your industry, your geographic targets, or other interests. There are too many to suggest favorites but some examples are IEEE.org (for electrical engineers), healthjobsusa.com (for healthcare jobs), indeed.com (can identify job openings within a 5-mile radius), seek.com.au (for jobs in Australia), workopolis.com (for jobs in Canada), hirediversity.com (specializing in diversity recruiting), eons.com, and grayhairmanagement.com (sites for those with more experience).

The online employment world is huge, and can be a major time vacuum. Do not cruise the Web looking for appropriate sites during the valuable 9-to-5 hours when it is most convenient to make personal contact with folks. If you are currently employed this goes double for you because it is hugely unwise as well as unethical to use your employer's computer or time to pursue these avenues.

The good news is that regardless of where these published openings are found, they all represent real jobs at real organizations that are looking to hire. The bad news is that any informed and motivated job hunter has access to the same job leads you do. As a result, this lowers your odds of landing any one particular job via this method. Some surveys say that published openings account for only 5 percent of the jobs filled annually in the United States. Other estimates are as high as 30 percent. But whatever tomorrow's statistics on this method are, it accounts for thousands and thousands of jobs. And just how many jobs are you looking for?

Traditional Sources: Cold Contacting

This is another traditional job-hunting method. From your library and online research, you identify a number of employers in your geographical target area that you think might need your skills. Using your research skills you identify the name of an appropriate line manager or human resources person to whom you send a cover letter and resume either by mail or e-mail. You do this a few places at a time, which allows you time to personally follow up on each letter. Within a given period of time (which you stated in your letter), you follow up with a phone call to make sure your resume was received and to see if any appropriate openings exist. It's as easy as that.

This method has somewhat fallen into disfavor because some people misuse it so badly. They take a huge, generic list, do a mass mailing to "whom it may concern," and then sit back and wait for something to happen. And usually nothing does. The only person to whom your job hunt may concern is you. Don't expect some unknown, faceless stranger to lurch out of nowhere and hire you. It just ain't gonna happen.

Used properly, targeted mailings can be a very effective way of uncovering leads in what has been referred to as the "hidden job market." There are a certain number of times that a resume just happens to cross someone's desk at the time a job opens up or is about to open up. Some estimate that targeted mailings may account for about 10 percent of the jobs filled annually.

Some employers prefer for job candidates to e-mail resumes directly to them at the company's own site. This is a great method because many organizations have software that can cross-reference your skills with openings they may have anywhere in the world. But don't abandon traditional ideas while trying out new ones; having a personal contact or endorsement will help get that e-mailed resume to the right person's desk.

Traditional Sources: Recruiters

There is an entire employee-recruiting industry devoted to helping organizations hire the right person for the right job. This industry, which some studies say accounts for 15 to 20 percent of yearly hires, is made up of temporary employment agencies, contracting agencies, contingency employment agencies, and retained executive search firms. Some of these companies will say they do all of the above, but common sense should tell you that makes about as much sense as having your dentist offer to do your colonoscopy. The best recruiters have specialties and are experts in one aspect of the employment industry. It's those folks with whom you want to be working.

Temp agencies (just as they sound) help organizations line up temporary help. Sometimes these temp assignments turn into full-time jobs; most of the time they do not. *Contract agencies* are similar to temp agencies, although the time frame and scope of the assignment are usually spelled out in greater detail. *Contingency employment agencies* (many also call themselves *executive recruiters*) generally help companies hire people at salary levels between $20,000 and $90,000. They get paid only if a job candidate they refer is hired (thus, their fee is "contingent"). Some are not very selective as to who they refer for interviews, whereas many others are quite professional. *Retained executive search firms* generally place executives at the $70,000 level and above. They are paid "on retainer" whether or not they fill the position. (Naturally, those firms that keep fees and don't fill positions don't stay around very long.) The best search firms are exceptionally selective because they guarantee to redo the search (a several-month process) if the selected candidate doesn't work out.

The way you get recruiters to help you during a specific job hunt is quite straightforward. Identify the recruiters who are specialists in your industry, who are in your functional area, and who work in your part of the world. Get this information from the annual *Directory of Executive Recruiters* (Kennedy Information) in your library's reference section, on the Web, in ads in professional publications, or with leads from your network. Send them a cover letter and resume alerting them to your availability. That's it. The end, finito, hasta la vista, baby. Don't call them; don't pester them with e-mails; don't drop in unannounced and offer to take them to coffee, lunch, drinks, or Disney World.

The best way to get your resume shredded by a headhunter is to be a pain in the butt. Why? Because recruiters *don't* find jobs for people. Recruiters find people for jobs. (Repeat these last two sentences until you understand them.) If you have the skills or background for an assignment that a headhunter is working on, she will be in touch with you. That's what headhunters do; that's how they make their living. If you have a particularly unique or interesting background, you may get a courtesy call to let you know that you're now in their database for future searches. But what they don't do is spend the day chatting with job hunters or giving career advice or trying to find you a job. It's just not the business they're in.

Some good news here is that no reputable employment agency or recruiter will ever charge you a fee. The hiring organization is the recruiter's client, and they pay the fee. Remember: I told you before that job hunting can be so hard that you can't even pay someone to do it for you. You may find that there are some crooks out there who will take your money and promise to find you a job—but they won't. Save your money. If you have an uncontrollable urge to throw your money away, feel free to send it to me. Of course, I won't find you a job either, but at least I won't lie to you about it!

Traditional Sources: Networking

So much has been written about networking that some tree-hugger types actually break out into tears whenever the term is used. Networking is made out to be a lot more complicated than it really is.

A quick definition may help. *Networking*: the process of asking people (some of whom you know and some of whom you'll meet along the way) to give you information that will be helpful to your job hunt. That's it.

Obviously, the big kahuna, the key piece of information you really want to find, is the name of the place where there is a great job ready and waiting for you. But the reality is that most people don't have that information for you. And if that's the only question you ask ("I'm looking for a job. Do you have any leads for me?"), then you will have totally wasted your network contacts. This is the biggest networking mistake job hunters make, and it can add months to a job search. They list their contacts, then go through the list checking off names as they call asking for job leads. They then sit back and say, "See? Networking doesn't work."

Your contacts have tons of really helpful information for you, but you have to know what it is and ask specifically for it. Most people are willing to help you, but you have to help them help you. You can ask and find:

* Names of places to look for published openings.
* Names of Websites that other job hunters have found useful.
* Great libraries or names of reference librarians who are especially knowledgeable or helpful.
* Local college, university, or alumni job-hunting resources.
* Names of recruiters working in your state, industry, or functional area.
* Locations of local job-hunting support groups.
* Names of growing/hiring local companies.
* How your resume looks; how your phone voice sounds.
* And, most importantly, who they know in their contact network who might be helpful to you in your job hunt.

This last item is especially important because you must be expanding your contact network continuously during the job hunt. You must never run out of people to contact; this is the biggest key to networking success. Start by listing every contact you can think of. (Use Tool #5, Building Your Contact Network, from the Toolkit.) Then, as you work your way through your contacts, you must train yourself to ask for the names of four or five people whom your contacts think may have some job-hunting–related information that could be helpful to you. This is essential to expanding your network.

Some of your contacts may resist, some may be very helpful right off the bat, and others you may have to spend some time educating about how the networking process works. You may need to call some back a second or third time to give them time to dig up some helpful information for you.

In almost 30 years of helping people change jobs and build careers, I have observed a somewhat counterintuitive phenomenon. I call it the "strength of weak ties." Most of your initial contacts will give you a lead or two, a piece of information, and maybe the names of one or two people to contact. This is a fine way to start. But I have observed that the further you build your network away from your first-level contacts, the more helpful people are: the more leads they share, the more ideas they generate, the more contact names they give you. I have a couple of assumptions about why this is true, but that's not important here. What is crucial to your job hunt is that you force yourself to build your network beyond your own personal contacts. That's where you will find the power of networking, and that is why study after study indicates that about 70 percent of the jobs filled annually are filled as a result of a contact made through networking.

New Tools/New Approaches

The four basic job-hunting methods haven't changed in a hundred years. But, thanks to rapid technological advances, some new tools can make the job search more productive—if you know how to use them. As with any new tool or approach there are some things to be wary of, and I'll mention them as well.

I. E-Mailing Resumes, Letters, and References

For starters I suggest setting up a separate e-mail account that you use only for job hunting. This is for privacy and security. It is far too easy to miss an important job search e-mail if it goes to your at-home or family e-mail address. Also, this gives you a chance to come up with a professional sounding address and get rid of surferboi411 or gothchick89. Never use your at-work e-mail address because your work e-mail does not belong to you; it belongs to your employer. If employed, remember to find and use the blocking feature that many online sites have so your employer doesn't learn that you are out there looking.

We are all familiar with the speed with which documents can be transmitted via the Internet. And anything that speeds up the job hunt is a blessing. For starters, identify yourself on the e-mail subject line. Make sure you have accurately labeled any documents you are attaching. I suggest a labeling format with your last name, first name, and what it is (for example, resume, cover note, references). Universal communication between systems has not yet been achieved, so you need to be sure whatever you are sending can be downloaded and read on the other end. You certainly don't want your resume to end up looking like hieroglyphics. One way to do this is to only attach documents that are in easily transferable typefaces such as Times New Roman and Arial.

A better and safer way to achieve this is to convert the document you're attaching to a PDF (Portable Document Format). This file format essentially takes a picture of your document that is easily transmittable, maintains its integrity, and can't be easily changed or edited by anyone else. Your Print function page has this option on it, or you can ask any fourth grader how to do it. Even if your e-mailed application or resume does not bounce back to you I suggest that you make a quick phone call to assure that your materials have been received.

II. Cell Phones and PDAs

These tools can keep you connected with the outside world 24 hours a day, seven days a week. This is a double-edged sword for all of us, and the job hunter is no exception. The obvious downside is the potential loss of privacy and having work (or your job search) intrude into your personal or family time. The benefit to the job hunter far outweighs any negative because these tools can greatly facilitate making contacts, scheduling meetings, arranging interviews, and following up.

DO:

* ✳ Set up your voice/text mail.
* ✳ Keep voice mails and text messages brief and business-like.
* ✳ Use someone else's phone to verify that your outgoing message is clearly audible and professional-sounding.
* ✳ Recharge your device daily.
* ✳ Check your phone/PDA voice mail and phone and text logs regularly.
* ✳ Make it a habit to turn off these devices prior to every meeting/interview.

DON'T:

* ✳ Answer or return a call or pick up messages from a moving vehicle or a noisy location.
* ✳ Engage in any conversation where you may be overheard.
* ✳ Pick up or respond to messages while waiting for a meeting or interview; use that time to focus on your strategy and goals for the meeting.
* ✳ Answer any call or respond to any message until you are sure of who it is from and you are prepared to respond positively and professionally.

III. Video Conferencing/Video Interviewing

As the cost of video conferencing technology has come down and the quality has improved, more organizations are using it in the hiring process. It is time-efficient, saves on travel expenses, and allows for the screening of more candidates and candidates from remote locations. If used effectively it can improve the quality of the interviewing and hiring process. Because it requires preparation, often a uniform set of questions is prepared that will be asked of all candidates, thus increasing the fairness of the process. Interviews can be recorded and reviewed later for a more accurate comparison of how candidates answered identical questions without relying on vague impressions, illegible notes, or faulty memories.

The hiring organization may use any number of video conferencing tools such as Skype, MSN Messenger, or Yahoo Messenger. Do not shy away from this process even if you are unfamiliar with it. There are many easy-to-find Websites that can guide you, and you can always ask the hiring organization for the instructions that they typically send to job candidates. If a recruiting firm has referred you to a potential employer it is likely that they have these tools on-site and will instruct you in their use.

Most up-to-date computers have video and voice capability, and it is probably the time to upgrade if yours does not. If this is impossible try to find a local employment center, college, library, family member, or friend that has a video-friendly computer you can use in privacy. Here are some ideas to help you master this technology.

BEFORE the video interview:

* Practice. Use your own Webcam or find someone else's to use to assess and adjust your overall appearance, demeanor, mannerisms, eye contact, lighting, and sound.

* Plan your attire as you would for any interview. Avoid busy patterns and stick to neutral colors.

* If interviewing from home, don't assume that only your top half will be seen. Also, remove from the camera's view anything that anyone might consider inappropriate for a business interview.

* Send any requested materials well in advance of the interview (resume, application form, portfolio pieces, and so on).

* Review any video instructions you've been given and feel free to ask for help with anything you don't understand.

✳ Clear your desk or workstation of clutter, distractions, and anything that might make noise or distract the interviewer.

✳ Arrange to be in place early to assure that everything is working and to relax a bit.

DURING the video interview:

✳ Feel free to ask for a quick review of the equipment.

✳ Ask if you can be clearly seen and heard.

✳ Confirm that they have any materials you have sent.

✳ Look at the camera; this is the video equivalent of eye contact. If you look down at your keyboard or desk all they will see is the top of your head.

✳ Don't panic if the system freezes up. Reboot your system and wait for them to call back. After five or 10 minutes you can try reaching them.

✳ Use the Picture-in-Picture feature, if your system has it, so that you can see what the other end is seeing.

✳ Don't fidget, play with paperclips, click your pen, or make any distracting noises the microphone will pick up.

✳ Use hand gestures sparingly.

AFTER the video interview:

✳ Do a post-interview review as you would with any interview. An invaluable tool for this, if your system has one, is a *record* feature.

✳ Plan for how you will improve your video interviewing performance.

✳ Send a thank-you note as you would for any interview.

The final points here should reinforce that a video interview is not much different from an in-person interview, but is just as important. I've heard it said that a video interview can be *more* important than a traditional, face-to-face screening interview because your performance can be reviewed, compared, and assessed more rigorously. Mastering this technology and this process is one more tool in your winning job interview toolkit.

IV. Blogging, Wikis, Webinars, and Twittering

These four methods of using technology to communicate with the world are not typically thought of as job-hunting tools even though each can have a significant effect on one's career prospects. You need to understand that any positive effect, such as raising your profile and acquainting others with who you are and what you have to offer, is apt to be long-term. On the other hand, you should also realize that a negative effect can be almost instantaneous if you risk damaging your image by presenting yourself in anything less than a mature, professional manner. If you are a novice with these methods, start off slowly, cautiously, and conservatively. If you are an experienced user don't forget that they can be like power tools: both incredibly effective and incredibly destructive. Let's look at each in turn.

A. Blogging

A blog (abbreviation of *Weblog*) is a Web-based journal in which you can establish yourself as an expert, commentator, or observer of the issues and topics in which you are most interested. It is often free to do so, and it is easy to set one up through such providers as blogger.com or wordpress.com. (There are dozens of providers and thousands of blogs; I advise you to scour the Web for positive role models before starting your own.) If you want to raise your profile in an area such as educational reform, socially conscious investing, or "green" business practices, you:

* Should have something worthwhile to say.
* Be open to accepting feedback both positive and negative.
* Be willing to post updates regularly to generate readership.

B. Wikis

Think of an electronic bulletin board where you can post information to be read, commented upon, or added to (think Wikipedia) by a restricted population, and you've got a pretty good idea of what wiki is.

Because it is not open to the entire Internet it is great for teams or task forces that share proprietary information, and may eventually make the traditional conference call obsolete. Setting up and running a wiki requires more Web know-how than a blog, so it is not for the novice, may require its own server, and should be run behind the corporate firewall. Want to learn more about wikis? Go to any number of Websites such as socialtext.com or wetpaint.com.

C. Webinars

Just as it sounds, a Webinar is a seminar conducted on the Web. It may be one-way (where you sit at your computer and listen, similar to a Webcast) or interactive, with capability for multiple presenters and/or questions and answers. It may be live or pre-recorded. It may be free, or you may be required to pay a fee to participate. Presenting or facilitating a quality Webinar is a good way of establishing your expertise in a field, and "attending" a Webinar may be a good way to quickly acquire some information you need. I must caution you here that some free Webinars are little more than infomercials, and there is almost no quality control or reference data on the Webinars that cost money, so one is often reduced to, as the old saying goes, "buying a pig in a poke."

D. Twittering

Depending on who you talk to, Twitter is either the biggest non-sensical time vacuum in the universe or the most powerful and fastest-growing social network the digital world has ever seen. Reality is somewhere between these two extremes, but any service that can grow 90 percent month over month demands notice.

I am not including Twitter in the next section on social networking because I think it is more accurate to call it a micro-blogging service (even though many of the caveats I outline for social networking sites are true for Twitter as well). Via Twitter, authors can send messages or updates of up to 140 text characters, which are called tweets, and are posted on the author's profile page. These messages can be sent to a restricted group known as followers, or, by default, can be viewed by anyone on the Web. Any user can send and/or receive tweets via the Twitter Website.

Much of what you find on Twitter supports the often dismissive comments about it being a frivolous waste of time. Many celebrities are hiring staff to pump out inconsequential tweets on an hourly basis to foster the illusion that you actually have some kind of relationship with them. Frankly, I don't care where my favorite musician or actor buys his socks or what he had for lunch. And if such gibberish isn't fodder for the stalkers out there then I don't know what is.

But if you know who you want to "follow" on Twitter, or what organization you want to gather real-time information about, or want to try to make a connection inside of a company where you currently have no contacts from your existing social network, then Twitter may be your new best friend. Again, as with all these techno tools and services, I urge you to explore and use Twitter only in the hours when personal or face-to-face contact is difficult or impossible. Only after becoming conversant with its usage do I suggest that you include it in your daily job-hunting regimen.

As this revised edition is being written, Twitter is beta testing an Adobe Air desktop application called TweetDeck. If its initial promise is realized it could become the personal browser of choice for millions of users. Not only could you connect with your contacts across multiple social networking sites, but you could also set up automatic updates about yourself, other people, industries (yours and others), professional fields (yours and others), products (yours and others), employers (yours and others), and any other topics of interest to you whenever they appear on Twitter. Ultimately it will include photo and video links. I have spoken to a handful of high-level marketing executives who indicate that TweetDeck is already changing the very nature of their jobs. Whether this will also be true for the job-hunting process remains to be seen, but it is a development that any wise professional will monitor with interest.

V. Social Media/Social Networks

Currently there are dozens of social networking sites, boasting users in the tens of millions. Some think that social networking will replace traditional job-hunting techniques because of its phenomenal growth and ubiquity. This is completely wrong, but social networking sites *are* valuable tools that can be used to more effectively and more rapidly pursue each of the four traditional job-search methods. You can use your online contacts to:

✳ Identify published openings.

✳ Initiate a cold contact with hiring managers or potential employers.

✳ Locate recruiters who work in your industry or function.

✳ Expand your existing network exponentially.

The wide-open forum that is the Web contains more material on social networking and job hunting than can be synthesized here. Further, it is hard to identify genuine user feedback. Some positive reports are little more than corporate viral marketing efforts. Some negative reports are merely the venting of disappointed job hunters who have learned that effective social networking actually requires knowledge, time, and energy. For this edition of *Winning Job Interviews* I interviewed or surveyed 112 job hunters in five countries who are actively using or have used social media to help them land a new job. The following results of my research do not represent the final word on this topic, but, rather, present a current snapshot of job hunters' experiences using social media to help them find employment.

✳ Some social networking sites are seen as "lighter," fun, or more recreational (for example, Facebook and MySpace) than sites such as LinkedIn and Plaxo that have a more professional or career orientation. (For example, Plaxo has just launched a new suite of tools called My Career that helps you search for jobs by key words such as title, company, skills, or location, has tips to help you strengthen your profile, can recommend jobs from more than 3 million postings to you based on your profile, and can import your contacts from other social media to help you build your professional network. This is what you would expect from a site that has a demographic that skews older, with a higher income, and the highest percentage of C–level executives.)

* "Friends" are not necessarily contacts who can or will help you. It is best to add contacts with whom you are really connected, who are aware of your background and capabilities, and who will positively reference you and refer you onward.

* After finding a job opening via any method it is a common strategy to search your social network(s) for those who might give you valuable insight into the organizational structure and culture, as well as anyone who might actually help you get in the door. This includes former employees, current employees, association executives, vendors, or suppliers.

* Human resources professionals and executive recruiters will frequently Google and check social sites to see what background information is available about job candidates. If they recognize a contact held in common it us not unusual for them to check out the candidate before ever speaking with him or her.

* Most job hunters indicated that it was more productive to start with a list of target employers and then search for contacts than to search for posted job openings.

* It is easy to get ignored if you contact someone you don't actually know. What helps is to do your homework first, see if you have a contact in common, and then have that person introduce you. Otherwise learn what you can. about them and their organization, and tailor your approach using this data.

* Consider posting a video resume on YouTube that you can forward to potential employers where you have uncovered an appropriate opening. Go to YouTube and view enough of them so that you can tell a good one from a bad one. Remember that it is not an autobiographical documentary; it is a short (two minutes at the most) presentation of what you can bring to the job and why you'd be great at it. If yours looks amateurish do not post it; work on it until it looks smooth and professional.

✳ There are four common social networking mistakes that can have disastrous effects on your job hunt and career. They are:

   ✳ **Writing about your employer or a former employer.** All potential employers see themselves as potential *former* employer, so *never* say anything negative about an employer. If you have or ever have had access to proprietary company information, never mention it, even if you believe it now to be in the public domain or are referring to it as part of a positive comment.

   ✳ **Posting or failing to remove silly, unprofessional, or inappropriate material from any of your profiles.** This is a public realm, not a private world that you have entered. Do not use unprofessional screen names. Be wary of posting information about your hobbies or recreational interests: That photo of you feeding an orphan might be helpful; the pic with the beer bong, not so much. You can do your best to delete harmful material, but a shadow always remains somewhere, and consider that any content you publish is on their servers, not yours.

   ✳ **Being on too many sites.** It is difficult to manage too many contacts in too many places, and it is easy to let your profile get out of date if it is posted on too many sites. It is as easy to spread yourself too thin on the Web as it is in real life. For some it is easier to spend time online talking about job searching than to actually conduct a job hunt on all fronts. At least for the duration of your job search consider dropping membership in any non-professional sites, such as The Doll Palace, Faceparty, or Vampire Freaks, unless it has some direct relationship to the job you are hoping to find.

✳ **Profile inaccuracies.** The top reason employers give for *not* hiring someone based on an Internet search is lying about one's professional background or job qualifications. The speed at which information travels today and the extent to which that information can be verified multiplies almost daily. If you are falsifying information it is not matter of *if* you will be found out, it is a matter of *when*. You may even be inventing something about which a potential employer cares little. But demonstrating untruthfulness is always a deal-breaker.

Each of the new tools and new approaches we've covered in this section is powerful all by itself. Taken together, they can markedly increase the effectiveness of any job search, and they can reduce the amount of time it take to uncover job leads and ultimately land a good job. But none of them is perfect. Each has its own unique strengths and limitations, and I have tried to be even-handed about both.

These new tools and new approaches reinforce the idea that the best use of the Web (for job hunters and non–job hunters alike) is to facilitate communication between people. This has been an essential requirement of the job search process for the last hundred years, and irrespective of any new and exciting technological development it will be an essential requirement of the job search process for the next hundred years.

MASTER THE PROVEN
FOUR-FRONT JOB CAMPAIGN

You now have a realistic set of goals for your job hunt, and you now know to use the complete array of job-hunting methods to effectively identify your job targets. What you need next is a road map, a game plan, to help you put it all together. I like the phrase *job campaign* because, similar to a military or political campaign, every activity is clearly linked to a specific, desired end result: you landing a great, new job.

Some job hunters start off by focusing on that one job-hunting method that was successful for them in their last job search. If the newspaper ads or a Website worked last time, they spend all their job-hunting time looking there. If a headhunter helped them last time, they call him or her and sit back waiting for the phone to ring. This makes a certain amount of sense, because if that method worked for you once, it was 100-percent successful—odds any job hunter would love.

Other job hunters, after reading a book such as this one, will apportion their time and energy according to the statistics of success for the various methods—for example, spending about 65 to 70 percent of their time networking, 15 to 20 percent of their effort working with recruiters, 10 to 15 percent of their energy cold-contacting potential employers, and 5 to 10 percent of their time tracking down published openings. This approach appeals to the systems folks among us, but I find it's best to remember Mark Twain's comment, "There are lies, damned lies, and statistics."

I have found that some job hunters will concentrate their time and energy using the single job-hunting method with which they feel most comfortable: in the library, on the phone calling recruiters, out there networking, in church lighting candles.

For most job hunters, and especially at the initial stage of your job hunt, this approach is *dead wrong!*

The fact is that you have no objective data about what job-hunting method will be successful for you during *this* job campaign. Since the time of your last job hunt, you have changed, the job market has changed, employers have changed, recruiters have changed, useful Websites have changed, libraries have changed, the technology of your job has changed—everything is different. What guided you to success last time may or may not work for you this time. That is why you need to <u>start off</u> your job campaign with equal energy on all four fronts.

Use Real-Time Feedback to Customize Your Job Hunt

Your job hunt is not a "one size fits all" deal. It needs to be tailored to what you're qualified to do, what you are looking for, and where you are looking for it. After a month or two of pushing your job campaign on all four fronts, you will begin to see what is working for you at this point in your career. You should begin (key word here: *begin*) to reapportion your time and energy accordingly. If your current skill set is now attracting more recruiters, spend a little more time with them. If your field is now doing a lot of employment advertising, spend some more time tracking down ads. But you must not abandon the other fronts in your campaign. To understand why, take a look at Figure 2.1 on the next page.

This diagram gives a good, brief overview of the job-hunting process: You use various methods to uncover potential job leads. When you find out there is a bona fide job opening, you enter the screening process; if there is a potential fit, you may be screened by phone or video; if that goes well, you may get into the interview process; if your interview(s) goes well, your references may be checked; next, you may get a job offer; if you negotiate effectively, you may get an even better offer.

However, if you want to get some real insight into what the job-hunting process is like, show this diagram to someone currently working hard in a job hunt. She will tell you that this illustration shows only a few of the ways a potentially good job lead can go south on you. Even with all the no's you see, it doesn't show the mail that wasn't delivered; it doesn't show the e-mail that got lost; it doesn't show the day your voicemail failed and you missed that important call; it doesn't show when you went to the wrong place for the interview or you ended up interviewing with the wrong person, or the right interviewer turned out to be an idiot, or the time you gave references who were not sufficiently prepared or who decided to tell all those funny stories about you, or the time, after you spent weeks doing everything right, they decided you were overqualified or too expensive, or the time that, for unknown reasons, the job you wanted so badly suddenly just "went away." This is what a seasoned job hunter will tell you about the job-hunting process, and it makes my next point.

Figure 2.1
Job Hunt Overview

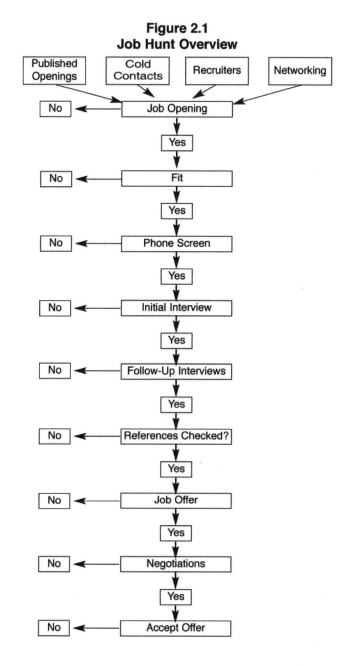

More Is Better

Job hunting is damn hard, it's unpredictable, and it can be very discouraging. But by understanding and managing the process, you can master it. This means you must continually use all job-hunting avenues at your disposal. Using only one or two job-hunting methods will make your job campaign harder and longer. Look again at Figure 2.1. If you want to succeed at this process with the least amount of stress and strain possible, you must continuously use all four major job-hunting methods to front-end load the system. More job leads are better, more phone screens are better, more interviews are better, and more offers are better. In the job-hunting process, more is always better. With more input, there will be more output. It's as simple as that.

Never Stop Starting

There is another common job-hunting mistake I want you to avoid. It is easy, especially if you've been at it for a while, to get overexcited about a particular job opportunity you uncover. It's with a great company, and you've heard from your contact inside the organization that it's a great place to work. You have passed the screening phase and are now ready to begin the interview process. You feel in your bones that this could be the one. Nothing is more typical than, at this point, putting all your eggs in one basket. I mean this in two ways: operationally and emotionally.

Realistically, you must face the fact that this job may or may not happen. Even if you are the greatest job hunter in the world and have the best interviewing skills in the world, there are tons of reasons why it might not happen. Thus, you must never stop starting the process. The more spadework you do to front-end load the job-hunting process, the better shape you will be in, operationally and emotionally, if one particular job doesn't pan out.

Even if you are going in for (what you hope is) your final interview, even if you already have an offer in hand, never stop starting. If this opportunity works out—great. You will have sounded more confident and maybe less willing to take whatever is offered to you because you have other opportunities in the pipeline. If this job falls through, at least you won't have lost a lot of time or inertia that you need to keep your job hunt moving forward.

Take another look at Figure 2.1. How would you feel if you uncovered only one job lead at a time, pursued it through the process up to a point where you didn't get it, and then had to go back to square one and start from scratch? You'd feel lousy—disappointed, discouraged, maybe hurt or angry, and certainly demotivated. This is a recipe for job-hunting failure if ever there was one. Now, think about going through this process a bunch of times. You'd be lucky to even get out of bed in the morning without thinking about jumping in front of a bus! One way to protect yourself emotionally during this process (which you remember from Chapter 1 is largely a process of rejection) is to always be working on something new, always have something else in the pipeline. You must never stop starting—until after you have started your new job.

Some of what we've discussed thus far hasn't exactly been all sweetness and light. Job hunting sucks—we all know that. Done correctly, it's a lot of work to get out there and conduct an effective, four-front job campaign to line up more and better interviews. But what comes next is where the tide turns in your favor. In Chapter 3 we're going to look at the most important person in the process: you. And we're going to talk about the control and power you have over this process, and how you can use it to your best advantage.

CHAPTER 3

YOU ARE IN CONTROL

One of the most important things you can learn about job interviewing is that you—yes, that's right, *you*—can exercise a remarkable degree of control over the entire process. Understanding, using, and expanding on the control you have over the interview may be the single most important factor in your ability to get the job you want and build it into a job you can love.

You may think, "Nonsense. After all, *they* read my letter or e-mail, *they* screened my resume, *they* listened to the headhunter, *they* talked to the person who referred me, and, ultimately, *they* called me to come in for an interview at *their* location and at a time of *their* preference. And, oh by the way, *they* will be asking the questions, *they* will determine if I'm the best job candidate, and *they* will decide if and when to make me a job offer. Exactly how does that put *me* in control?"

I wish I could tell you that I'm about to teach you the secret of the Vulcan Mind Meld so you could open up the interviewer's mind like a ripe melon, pluck out whatever you wanted, and bend him to your every whim. If I ever figure that one out, I'll let you know. But until then, you will have to be satisfied with the proven techniques and approaches I have learned from thousands of successful job hunters who have used them to take charge of their job interviews and land a job they love.

WHY CONTROL IS
IMPORTANT TO YOU

Some folks just attract other people to them. I'm not talking about physical attractiveness here; I'm talking about personal traits such as friendliness, courtesy, genuine interest in the other person, good listening skills, and an ability to influence the environment rather than being driven or controlled by it. These qualities are essential to improving your winning interview performance.

A person who radiates a sense of control communicates competency, calm, and confidence. Your interviewing goal is to communicate that you are the best person for the job in question, and all three of these traits are essential to that goal.

A person who goes into an interview with a sense of control contributes to a climate of certainty, predictability, or lowered risk. These are subtle qualities all interviewers are looking for (though many don't even know it). Someone who feels not in control seems passive, not active; more of a follower than a leader; someone who doesn't stand out from the crowd.

No matter how subtly you feel it, a sense of powerlessness will work against you in your interview. When you feel not in control, it does not help you present yourself, either personally or professionally, in a way that attracts other people. And all of these factors are essential for you to deal with if you want to emerge from that interview as the leading job candidate.

Now, let's put the list together: You need to be competent, confident, certain, predictable, action-oriented, and attractive on both a personal and professional level. These are the very qualities that will lead you to winning job interviews and that will ensure your success in your new job. Here's how you get them.

COMMUNICATING
CONTROL

By "taking control" I do not mean charging into the interviewer's office like a star from World Wrestling Entertainment, physically overwhelming the space with your body language and cologne while verbally dominating the conversation by not letting the interviewer get a word in edgewise. It might be kind of fun to watch, but it sure as heck won't get you the job.

It has been stated—and with some fairness, I think—that what is seen as legitimate assertiveness in some men can be seen as aggressiveness in some women. You've heard it before, I'm sure. He's "take charge"; she's "bossy." He "looks out for his people"; she's "territorial." He can be a "pain in the neck"; she's a "pain in the..."—well, you get the picture. In an increasingly diverse working world, these attitudes may seem Neanderthal to you and me both, but my counsel is to ignore them at your peril.

Two things I am absolutely certain about are that (a) you *do* want to exhibit the appropriate level of assertiveness in the interview in order to demonstrate that you can completely fulfill the requirements of the job you're seeking, and (b) you *do not* want to cross the invisible (and sometimes gender-biased) line between assertiveness and aggression. There are three steps to managing this balancing act. They are: get smart, get feedback, and get ahead.

Get Smart

Women's and men's conversational styles differ in many ways, and how we converse with each other at work is how we get stuff done: planning, cooperating, coaching, directing, selling, disciplining, leading. Improving your interpersonal communication style and understanding how others may be perceiving you are essential skills in today's world of work. Our conversational skills are constantly being evaluated at work and are scrutinized minutely under a microscope during the job-interview process.

Resources abound to help you increase your knowledge and skills of communication. Regarding gender differences in communications, I strongly recommend the book *Talking From 9 to 5: How Women's and Men's Conversational Styles Affect Who Gets Heard, Who Gets Credit, and What Gets Done at Work* (William Morrow, 1994) by Dr. Deborah Tannen, who is a leader in this field. Dr. Tannen has had other best-sellers on this topic, but this one is a must for the bookshelf of any manager or job hunter.

My next recommendation might surprise you a little bit. One of the best general texts I've found on how to improve your communication skills is *How to Talk So Kids Will Listen & Listen So Kids Will Talk* (Perennial Currents, 1999) by Adele Faber and Elaine Mazlish. I've had a number of clients tell me that Faber and Mazlish's ideas for improving their listening (and understanding) skills, dealing with feelings, and encouraging both autonomy and cooperation were just as useful at work as they were at home. Communication skills that make you a winner at work are certain to make you irresistible as a job candidate. Thus, making the effort to improve your skills in this area will generate concrete benefits during this and every other stage of your career.

Get Feedback

The problem with any book is that it is one-way communication. I can talk to you, but you can't talk back to me (at least not in any way I can hear). I have no effective way of assessing your communication style—whether it is too loud or too soft, too laid back or too domineering, too indirect or too in your face. I have no way to offer you remedial actions or improvement ideas. You need real feedback, and here's how to get it:

1. Take a moment to look at the Energy Level/ Communication Effectiveness Model in Figure 3.1 on the next page. It shows how communicating with too much or too little energy can negatively affect how you communicate.

Figure 3.1

**Energy Level/Communication
Effectiveness Model**

2. Because you are one of the best sources of information about yourself, ask yourself the following questions:
   a. When do I communicate in the passive zone?
   b. When do I communicate in the assertive zone?
   c. When do I communicate in the aggressive zone?
   d. In what zone do I most frequently communicate?
   e. In what zone do I most frequently communicate when I'm interviewing?
3. Find some other sources of feedback. Ask a couple of trusted (and honest!) friends or colleagues the same five questions you asked yourself in number 2. Search your old performance reviews for clues. Who else has data you could gather, who else knows you well—a mentor, a counselor, a former coworker?
4. Write down these impressions and see how they coincide or conflict with your self-assessment. Finally, compile an overall assessment of the energy level you most frequently use when communicating.

Get Ahead

If you have determined that you are predominantly a passive or an aggressive communicator, you will need to make some major changes. Not to worry—very few people are born with precisely fine-tuned communication skills, and there are many readily available steps you can take if you really want to develop winning job interview skills.

Let's say you have figured out that you are too passive in the way you communicate with others. This is bad news because no job interviewer is going to sit there and try to pry information out of you. He might think you're not overly interested in the job, not "good with people," painfully shy, hungover, or who knows what else. But, in any event, you will not stand out as a winning job candidate.

On the other hand, maybe you have determined that you are much too aggressive in the way you communicate with others. This is also bad news because you will be seen as hard to work with, a know-it-all, not a team player, or domineering. No interviewer is going to recommend hiring you if you come off as an angry, opinionated loudmouth, unless you're looking for a job as a radio talk show host.

If you want to improve your skills in either of these areas, here are a few ideas you can use:

* ✳ See if your current employer offers any in-house workshops in communication skills or assertiveness training.

* ✳ Go to your human resources department and see what information they have about interpersonal skills workshops or assertiveness training seminars offered locally. Find out if your employer will pay for all or part of it. Many do.

* ✳ Call your local community college and look up what courses or workshops they offer in this area. (Tuition is often very low, and you can either use it as a tax deduction, or your employer may reimburse you.)

* ✳ Use your Yellow Pages or the Web to find your local Toastmasters International chapter. Start attending their meetings and I guarantee you'll enjoy it.

WHOSE INTERVIEW
IS IT, ANYWAY?

I want you to actually stop for a minute or two to think about this question. Sure, your potential employer is interviewing you, but she is probably interviewing other folks as well. This makes the time you are there *your* interview. It's *your* time to sell your skills and background; it's *your* time to be seen as a winner; it's *your* time to shine. This interview is *yours*, and I want you to take responsibility for it.

I don't care if you're being interviewed by the biggest dope on the planet, you can (subtly, of course) control the flow, the atmosphere, most of the content, and sometimes even the actual outcome of your job hunt by learning the interviewing secrets you'll find in this chapter. In almost 30 years of working as a psychologist in a variety of different settings (executive coach, outplacement consultant, executive recruiter, and career counselor), I've discovered how the most anxious, tentative job hunter can learn to be a winning job interviewer.

By taking personal responsibility for your interview, you will start to assert control over it. And you will learn to take control of it by doing three things:

1. You will go into your interview with the right attitude.
2. You will go into your interview with the right knowledge of the process.
3. You will go into your interview with the right preparation.

We will cover attitude and knowledge now and devote the entire next chapter to preparation.

THE RIGHT
ATTITUDE

If you are a human being, your emotions affect how you behave. How you behave influences how others around you behave. Thus, going into your job interview with the right attitude can affect how you

behave and how the interviewer behaves, and will influence the outcome of the interview. If you go into an interview with a hat-in-hand
attitude or a "please sir, I need this job" attitude, you will undercut the
positive impression you're trying to make. However, if you go into
your interview with an upbeat, "this is a great opportunity for both of
us" attitude, you will make a much stronger and more positive impression of yourself as a person and of your professional capabilities. We
have already touched on one way for you to develop the right interviewing attitude—that is, by understanding whose interview this is, by
knowing who owns this interview: you. Let's look at a few more ways
to make this happen.

The Wind Is in Your Favor

You have psychology working for you because the interviewer
assumes, more or less, that you can do the job. That's right! You're not
going in with a blank slate; you're going in with an assumption in your
favor. In today's hectic world, no one has the spare time to interview
someone they think *can't* do the job, do they? Only the best candidates, only the most appropriately skilled individuals, only those folks
whom the interviewer actually *hopes* can do the job are being interviewed. Of course, it's up to you to communicate that you actually
can do the job, but, in reality, the interviewer is already part of the
way there.

This Isn't *Dragnet*

The interview is a two-way street. You're not going in to be grilled
like a hot dog on the 4th of July, nor are you going to be interrogated
like an enemy agent in some war movie. (On a rare occasion you may
run into some moron who thinks he'll run you through a "stress" interview. Don't worry about that for now. We'll cover that later, in Chapter
8.) You are going in for a business meeting, one where business information is sought and offered on a two-way street. They have work that
needs to be done and the money to pay for it. You have the skills and
attitude that can get that job done. They are trying to determine if you
are the best person for them, and you are trying to find out if this is the

best place for you to work at this point in your career. A good interview is a professional meeting to determine if two parties can come to an agreement in their mutual best interest. It is not a situation in which one side has all the power.

You Have a Real Edge

You probably know more about the interviewing process than the interviewer does. If you read this book from cover to cover and learn only half of what I've put in here for you, you will have a better handle on the interviewing process than 90 percent of the interviewers you will run into. More than a dozen nationwide corporate training companies have verified what I have discovered in my own consulting practice: some of the least-attended management training courses or seminars are those on interviewing skills for hiring managers. I'm told that the reason is that most hiring managers have been interviewed themselves on any number of occasions so they think they know how to do a good job at it. I'm here to tell you that most of them do a lousy job of interviewing. This is bad news for them but good news for you, because I'm going to teach you what they don't know, and what they don't know will help you knock that interview out of the park.

It's Like Skydiving

In job interviewing (like skydiving) you don't get a do-over if you blow it on the first try. You never get a second chance to make a first impression. So, how do you go into an interview (often a first meeting) and have it look and feel as if you're a seasoned, comfortable professional? The answer is by thorough preparation and leaving nothing to chance.

Preparing for the interview will immeasurably improve your attitude, build your confidence, and enhance the way you present yourself. Because this is so important, we will spend an entire chapter on the easy-to-follow steps that you can take to prepare effectively for your interview. (Unfortunately, most job candidates' preparation for a job interview consists of getting a good night's sleep.) But for now, the point is that by the very fact that you take the time to actively prepare for the interview, you will go into it with more poise, more thoughtfulness, and more confidence—a winning combination if ever there was one.

Why Are You There?

I want you to walk into that interview knowing exactly why you are there. Having a crystal-clear goal foremost in your mind will improve your interviewing attitude immensely. If the interview is a screening interview, your goal is to get called back. If it is a group interview, your goal is to personally connect with as many people in the group as possible. If it is a final interview, your goal is to close the deal and get the job offer. Most people go into an interview with the idea that they will "see what happens" or "hope for the best." Not you. With my help, you're going in to win!

THE RIGHT
KNOWLEDGE

Knowledge is power, in interviewing as well as in the rest of life. The job-interview process is where the interviewer discovers things about you: details about your education, your working relationships, your previous assignments, your career aspirations. It is *not*, however, the correct venue for you to be discovering things—either about the organization with the job opening or about the interview process itself.

That is all knowledge you should have brought to the interview with you, to help you tailor your answers and your follow-up questions, and to improve your overall presentation. Sure, you should be in there actively listening and picking up on new information, but you shouldn't be in there in basic research mode. I don't want you in there trying to find out stuff your competition is walking in the door with. I want you in there sharing new ideas, explaining how you plan to contribute—selling yourself. I want you walking into that interview knowing more about your potential employer than all the other candidates. I also want you walking into the interview better prepared than all the other candidates by completely understanding the dynamics of the interview process itself. By doing these things, you will walk out of the interview a winner.

Back to Your New Best Friend

In the last chapter I introduced you to your new best friend, your reference librarian. Not only can this person help you in setting your overall job-hunting goals, but she will also be invaluable in the critical phase of interview preparation.

You want to arrive for an interview with a boatload of information. What do you know about the organization where you are asking to spend months and maybe years of your life? What do you know about its products or services? What do you know about its reputation, its history, its various locations, its financial health? Why is this job open? What challenges do you think will face the person who fills this job opening? These are only a few of the questions you should be asking yourself before you present yourself for the interview.

Having answers to all of these questions will help distinguish you from the other job candidates during the interview process in a number of very important ways.

✳ The most obvious benefit is that, by knowing more about the organization, you are better equipped to sell yourself into it by matching your skills with its needs.

✳ By knowing more about the organization, you can more easily establish a common vocabulary with the interviewer, and that facilitates the overall level of communication.

✳ You are demonstrating that the job-hunting and interviewing process is of prime importance to you and that you are willing to invest the time and energy to succeed at it.

✳ You will subtly communicate that you are hardworking, serious, thorough, and curious—not to mention knowledgeable.

These are qualities for which every potential employer is looking, and demonstrating them will put you in the first tier of job candidates.

You also want to learn as much as you can about the interviewer himself. Any common ground you can find will help you, especially during those first awkward stages of establishing a relationship. Do you know any people in common? Has anyone in your network ever worked with this person? Do you belong to any organizations in common? Has he ever made any presentations that you can access or has he written anything you can read? Have you Googled the interviewer to see what else there might be to learn? An obvious (I hope) caution here is to use any personal information that you uncover sparingly, because nobody wants to hire a stalker!

Pick Up on the Rhythm

Every interview has a predictable rhythm. Listening for and understanding this rhythm is easy once you are aware of it. It will give you valuable feedback (during the interview itself) that will help you know how you are doing and help you get a better sense of where you are in the process. You can use this knowledge to fine-tune your approach even as the interview is underway. Let's take a quick look at Figure 3.2.

Figure 3.2

Interview Process Overview

This model gives you an easy way to look at two important aspects of job interviewing. The top line goes from start through middle to finish. This represents the progress you make going through an individual interview. The bottom line goes from screening to selecting. This represents where you are in the overall interview process. You will note from the model that both aspects of the interview have much in common.

As an organization begins to evaluate you (during the screening process) it needs to confirm that you and the other candidates the organization plans to invite in for interviews can, in fact, do the job. That means verifying that you have the experience, skills, and knowledge to do the job. To figure out if you are still in the screening process or if you have moved forward to the selection process, just consider the questions you are asked on the phone or in person. If the focus is primarily on experience, skills, and knowledge, you are still in the screening process. If the focus is primarily on who you are as a person (your personal qualities, your family, your outside interests, and the like), then you have moved on to the selection process.

This insight also helps you determine where you are in any individual interview. Most interviewers go into the process with an agenda; it might not be an organized one or a particularly effective one, but they usually have *some* basic game plan. After a few opening pleasantries, typically, they will move to their agenda. Once they have attempted to learn what they need to know, they will often move on to softer, more personal questions that focus on who you are as a person. You need to observe this closely because these questions can give you important information as to how you are doing, and also give strong clues as to exactly what it is they are looking for.

You Can See the Future

If I've heard it once, I've heard it hundreds of times. It's a nervous job interviewee saying that she hates being put on the spot, that she's not very spontaneous, and that she can never think of the best way to answer questions when she's under pressure. If only she had the interviewer's list of questions ahead of time. Then she could calmly and reflectively come up with the best, most interesting way to portray her background. She wouldn't be floundering around in the hot seat.

Some think I've blown a gasket when I tell them that they have at their disposal a tool that will predict 80 to 90 percent of the interview questions they will ever be asked. They really start to wonder when I say that this tool, at this very moment, is somewhere on their desk or in their briefcase or in the job-search folder in their computer. Can you guess what this secret weapon is?

This secret weapon is your updated resume. You have written your resume so that it highlights all the great things you've done, all your accomplishments, all the wonderful stuff you want to talk about. (I mean, nobody's resume has negative stuff on it such as, "Rolled the delivery van, cost the company $15,000.") Your resume is a sequential road map through all the places you've worked. It details all your relevant education and training. In short, it has tons of positive information that you want your interviewer to hear.

Your resume presents you with a golden opportunity to put an interview outline you have designed, with data you have chosen and want to be asked about, directly into the hands of your interviewer. The key to using this secret weapon is to know this information in complete detail—backward and forward and inside out.

Sure, a few questions may come from left field, but most of them will stay pretty darn close to the data you have chosen to present, and (here's more good news) you will have had all the stress-free time in the world—before the interview—to come up with accurate and insightful answers to any of them.

Turning Good Into Great

In the next chapter we'll delve more deeply into preparing specific answers to questions. What I'd like you to do now is set some really high expectations for your interviews. I don't want them to be just good; I want them to be great. When you walk out of the interviewer's office I want him to say, "Boy, I enjoyed that. What an interesting person. I hope we can get her to work here." Here's one way to turn good interviews into great interviews.

I want you to take each little item on your resume—that's *every* item—and justify why it's there. It should say something great about you. If it's boring, edit it out. If it highlights one of your strengths, it's in. Then, for every remaining resume item, I want you to come up with an interesting story about it. Dry facts don't sell. Interesting, engaging stories sell. You want to fill your interview with engaging, interesting stories that highlight all the wonderful things you can bring to a new employer. Regardless of one's religious beliefs, it's easy to see that Jesus' ability to tell powerful but simple stories about the most basic things in life (they were called "parables") is one of the reasons that a tiny sect grew into one of the most powerful movements the world has ever known. Now, I'm not expecting you to convert the world. I just want you to bring a few interviewers into your flock.

Your Fail-Safe Backup Plan

You, my astute job candidate, may ask, "Okay. So I can predict most of the questions I'll get asked. What about the 10 to 20 percent that I can't predict?" (We're not talking about doofus questions here. Occasionally you may get the bozo who asks who your favorite kid in the Brady Bunch was. We'll have some fun with the topic of idiot interviewers in Chapter 8.) I'm talking about a question that clearly relates to the job you're hoping to land, but somehow you didn't see it coming. Not to worry. Dr. Paul has a fail-safe answer for you, and it's a great one at that. All you have to do is understand and remember the equation in Figure 3.3 on the next page.

Whether you know it or not, every interview question you are asked is actually a two-part question. The first part is the hard data: your experience, your knowledge, your skills. It is designed to answer the question "Can he do the job?" The second part is the soft data: your personal characteristics, your personality, who you are as a person. How would your doing the job be different from anybody else's doing the job? It is designed to answer the question, "Of all the qualified candidates, is she the one that fits best with the rest of the organization?" No matter what interview question you are asked, whether or not you have a prepared answer, you need to hit both of these chords. This is not only a fail-safe answer for an unexpected question, it is

Figure 3.3

Dr. Paul's Fail-Safe Interview Answer Formula

[Ex + Kn] + [PC] = Fail-Safe Answer

Ex = Experience
Kn = Knowledge
PC = Personal Characteristics

another way to think about turning a good answer into a great answer for any question.

Part one (knowledge and experience) without part two (personal characteristics) gives an answer that is flat and impersonal. That answer will only tell how *anybody* would do the job if they had the right background; it doesn't help *you* stand out from the crowd. Part two (personal characteristics) without part one (knowledge and experience) is too generic and too vague; it doesn't address the basic issue of job performance that must be answered, and it will sound as if you're trying to sell yourself into a job for which you may not be qualified.

Using this easy-to-remember equation will help you generate a strong answer to any interview question, one that supplies the confirmation that you have the hands-on skills and background to do the job, as well as the personal qualities that make you an enjoyable teammate and someone with whom others will prefer to work.

By now you have learned that the job interview belongs to you: It is yours to control, yours to win, or yours to blow. We have taken a look at two of the major ways you can take control of it: by developing the right attitude and by gaining essential knowledge of the process. Now let's move on to Chapter 4, where I will show you an easy-to-follow plan that will help you prepare thoroughly and professionally for any interview and dramatically increase the odds that you will land the job you really want.

CHAPTER 4

BUILDING YOUR WINNING INTERVIEW PLAN

I have heard people refer to a job interview as an audition or a command performance. Some think that this belittles the process by comparing it to mere entertainment as opposed to the serious business of landing a job you love. I do not.

True performers don't just go out on stage to see what will happen next. They plan, they prepare, they practice, and they leave nothing to chance. Sure, there are some performers who improvise more than others (jazz musicians and comedian/actor Robin Williams come to mind), but even they are working with a plan, within a certain structure, and with a definite end point in mind. This is how I want you to be prepared for your job interviews: relaxed but focused, prepared but not robotically programmed, ready to shine, and with your eyes on the prize.

Anxiety and stress do, indeed, affect performance, but they are not bad things in and of themselves. They are the way our bodies and our minds tell us that we are in a situation of some risk—a job interview, for example. In fact, a certain, moderate amount of stress can give you the extra edge (that is, heightened awareness, alertness, responsiveness) that can help you turn a good interview into a great interview. The exhilarated feeling you have after you've left an interview where you did really well is, in fact, this adrenaline at work.

For many people, however, the anxiety and stress brought on by an interview can be a real problem. Some get so nervous that they forget basic, boilerplate information about themselves—such as their name! Or they get so tongue-tied that they can barely squeak out a yes or no answer. I want you to reduce, but not completely eliminate your interview anxiety. I want you comfortably relaxed, but not so chilled out that you come across as laissez-faire or uninterested. On the other hand, I still want you to maintain that edge, that look in your eye that says, "I know this is an important meeting and I'm up for it because I'm well prepared." Energized and confident, but not cocky. There are a host of ways to achieve this vital balance. Let's focus first on some of the practical and tactical issues that are so often overlooked.

LOOKING AND FEELING
YOUR BEST

Professional, attractive, comfortable. These three qualities should be the hallmarks of your personal presentation at your interview. They apply to your interview outfit, your shoes, your haircut, your mustache, beard, or goatee, your eyeglasses, your bag (purse or briefcase), your pad and pen, and anything else the interviewer can see. Remember: this person has only a limited amount of time (a few hours at best) to decide if he wants to spend some number of months and years with you, so he is looking for any piece of data from which he can draw assumptions about you.

Your Arrival

I think it was Woody Allen who said that showing up is 80 percent of life. I think the number goes considerably higher if we're talking about job interviews. There may be some uncertainties about your interview, but one thing we know for a fact is that it ain't gonna happen if you ain't there! You need to know exactly where your interview is, exactly how to get there, and exactly how long it will take to get there. One of the worst ways to start an interview is to come racing in the door, late, making excuses and offering apologies.

Don't rely on any single source of data to locate your interview. Call and ask the receptionist for directions and check that she is actually familiar with the route you will be taking. If you're using public transportation, talk to someone who is actually familiar with the system and knows the stops. If using directions downloaded from the Web, check more than one source, because, as wonderful as these can be, they also can be off by as much as a hemisphere. Check the Website of the organization you're interviewing with to see if it has directions posted. (I have found these to be the best.)

If practical, make a test run to your interview site. Do this at the same time of day as your interview. This is good data to have in the event that you are offered the position and you need to figure out how long your new commute will be. These points may seem minor now, but, together, they all will contribute to your looking, feeling, and doing your best in the interview.

Your Outfit

You need two or three interview outfits. Have an objective, professional friend give you some honest feedback about which of your outfits work best. (If you are working with a recruiter, she can give you some excellent input.) If you need to update your wardrobe, hey, it's the cost of doing business. Just make sure to wear the outfits a few times to break them in before your interview. You don't want a stray pin, dangling thread, underwire, or scratchy label make you twitch around in your seat. This goes double for new shoes that may squeak, slip, or make you walk funny.

Much has been made of the new, more casual look in the workplace. Because I truly believe that neckties are tools of the devil (and I'm told pantyhose are as well), I'm all for the casual look. But the casual look is for people already *on the bus*. You are *not* on the bus. The interview process is for them to see whether or not they *let you* on the bus. I don't care if the dress code at your potential new employer is

Hawaiian shirts and bunny slippers. You show up for your interview dressed professionally. You can always remove your jacket or loosen your tie if asked to, but you want to communicate that this is an important enough meeting for you to do whatever it takes to make a positive impression.

Once you're comfortable with your interview outfits, have them cleaned and pressed, and keep them separate from the rest of your clothes. You want to have them ready to go at the drop of a hat in case you suddenly get that interview call you've been waiting for.

Your Grooming

This quick section should almost go without mention. Almost. Except that I've seen people show up for interviews with haircuts that look like they were done by Stevie Wonder. I've been told of senior managers who showed up for interviews smelling as if they had been held hostage for a month in a garlic warehouse. And, on one occasion, I actually had to open a window so I wouldn't gag on petroleum fumes because this executive had spilled gasoline all over his shoes at a self-service station on his way to my office. (For Pete's sake, either get your gas the day before or spring for the extra 2 cents a gallon to have it pumped for you!) Do any of these single idiosyncrasies mean that the candidate cannot do the job? No. Can any of these single idiosyncrasies stick in an interviewer's head and ultimately work against you? Yes. Sorry, pal. I didn't make up these rules; I'm just trying to help you win by understanding them.

Men: You don't need a manicure, but do invest in a nailbrush and clippers.

Women: Your job interview isn't the time or place to test-drive that new Goth Princess makeup kit.

Haircut rules: Neat, presentable, and in a color frequently associated with human beings. This is not the time to make a fashion statement unless the statement is "I'm great; I'm normal; please hire me."

You can't walk down a city street (or watch an NBA game) these days without noticing the growing number of tattoos, piercings, nose rings, and other body art. The trip to some beaches is even scarier.

My advice is: If you have this stuff, keep it covered or remove it when interviewing because it can work against you. If you are hired, you can gradually start displaying, safety-pinning, or clipping on whatever you choose—at least until someone complains to the boss. There are alternative workplaces (such as bars, music stores, entertainment venues, and such) where this is a nonissue. But most organizations that deal with the public or work with other businesses aren't that interested in hiring someone who looks as if he's been rolling around in a tackle box. If this is where you want to make your big existential stand and say, "This is how I am. They can hire me or not," then so be it. Just be clear that you might be trading off a paycheck for a nose ring.

Your Stuff

You don't want to trudge into your interview burdened down with a bunch of stuff, making you look like a Sherpa heading up Mount Everest. Stash your hat, coat, umbrella, galoshes, and change of shoes (if necessary) in a closet in the lobby or lunchroom. Try to find a rest room to comb your hair or give yourself a once-over.

One bag—that's it. That's all you bring in. There are some nice briefcases available that aren't all that expensive; if yours is beat up, go get a new one. Do not use the grungy backpack that you take to the gym. If you are a woman, your briefcase will need to be a bit bigger to accommodate the essentials from your purse. This looks more professional than having a bag swinging from each shoulder like Gunga Din.

You need to have a pad of paper and a couple of working pens (no chew marks, please) with which you can take notes if you need to. You should have a couple of file folders: one with some extra copies of your resume and one with some copies of the list with your job references. If you are an artist or designer of some sort, you may need to have some portfolio pieces with you to show.

What else?

Jewelry: Keep it to a minimum, nothing jangling or distracting.

Wristwatch: Something business-like (no cartoon characters), with the alarm turned off.

Aftershave, cologne, or perfume: If you must, wear only the slightest hint, because many folks are allergic.

Breath mints: These are always a good idea, as is brushing your teeth (just try to keep that stupid tie out of the sink).

Makeup: This isn't a fashion show or nightclub, subtle works best.

Eyeglasses: No shades, no tinted lenses, and clean the leftovers from lunch off of the lenses.

Electronics: Before you enter the building, double check to make sure cell phones and other electronics are silent or, preferably, turned off.

Your Smile

There is nothing more attractive than a smile. Books have been written, poems have been recited, and songs have been sung about the power of a smile. Practice one right now. Feels good, eh? Your smile is an invaluable tool that you must remember to take with you and use in your interviews.

I know that you're a little tense, you're hoping to do your best, and you're trying to remember all the great answers that you have so thoroughly prepared. But when most of us are deep in thought, we don't smile; we frown. You've got to change this, and you can do it with practice. (We'll talk more about this later.)

When you smile at someone the natural reaction is for him or her to return your smile. A smile is one of the very first building blocks in a relationship, and that's what you are trying to accomplish in your interview: to build a relationship with your interviewer. You want to communicate that you are an open, communicative, engaging, and willing partner in this process. Remembering to smile will help you immeasurably.

Your Attitude

When you arrive for your interview—for your *winning* interview— I want you to have a positive, winning attitude. Smiling will help improve your attitude, but there's a little more work to do than just that. By making the effort to prepare thoroughly for your interview, you will have reduced your stress. By practicing your interviewing skills, you will have additionally eased your interview anxiety. What else can you do?

The answer to this question varies from person to person, and there is no one-size-fits-all answer. If you carry your stress in your body, then exercise, such as a bike ride, a walk, or a jog, can help. If you tend to be a worrier or carry your anxiety around in your head, then watching a movie, reading, reciting a prayer, or meditating can help. Maybe what will help you most is a combination of a couple of different approaches. But choose some specific, positive activity to improve your interviewing attitude because it is a key factor in how you will be perceived.

QUESTIONS AND ANSWERS

In Chapter 3 you learned some very important things about the questions you will be hearing in your job interviews. The vast majority of them can be answered with data that comes right off of your resume, which is why it is so important that you have a great resume and that you know it inside and out. A few of those who interview you may not have your resume in front of them. Some of the best interviewers I've ever seen make a list of their questions ahead of time on a separate piece of paper, and, assuming most of what is on your resume is genuine, put it away and only include one or two things from your resume that they want to explore in detail. If you find yourself in this situation, I want you to not just offer, but actually hand over one of the copies of your resume that you brought with you. Most interviewers will not decline it, and, with some luck, you're back to their using the interview map of your design as their map to your winning job interview. Again, it is essential for you to have an interesting story to tell that illustrates every single item on that document.

In Chapter 3 you also learned that those questions that do not come directly from your resume can be answered with the judicious use of Dr. Paul's Fail-Safe Interview Answer Formula (Figure 3.3). There are dozens of questions that are asked time and time again.

I have listed more than a hundred of the most popular ones for you in Tool #6, Frequently Asked Interview Questions. Ultimately, I want you to prepare answers for each of them and use them in your practice sessions. For now, the way to start is by taking the time to completely think through two things:

1. What is it that the interviewer is hoping to learn about you?

2. What is it that you want to make sure the interviewer learns about you?

Most of the time there is a great deal of overlap between these two areas. But in case the interviewer doesn't do a great job of discovering how wonderful you are, it is *up to you* to make sure this message gets across. These two categories could account for about a million different questions and answers, and there's no way anyone could ever prepare for them all. Fortunately, there is a tool that you can use to organize your interview preparation. Consider Figure 4.1 on the next page. In the following sections we'll talk through each of the circles shown.

"I'LL TAKE THE CATEGORY
HIRE ME FOR 400, ALEX"

My reading tastes are pretty eclectic, and, having a mind that retains tons of useless information, I once read a book by Alex Trebek about the TV show *Jeopardy!* In it he mentions how some big *Jeopardy!* winners prepare themselves. They don't randomly read book after book or peruse the encyclopedia; instead, they take the time to think through which categories might appear and dig into them one by one (for example, mountain ranges, Shakespearean tragedies, and, my favorite, potent potables). Using this technique we can successfully predict the categories of questions you will be asked, and you can systematically begin to organize your preparation for the interview itself.

Figure 4.1

Interview Preparation

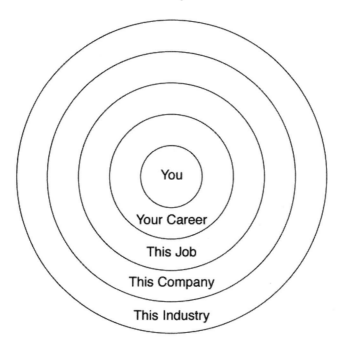

You

Granted, this category is large. The way to narrow it down is to ask yourself what you would need to learn about a job candidate as an individual before hiring her. You would want to learn where she is from, where she went to school, what she studied and why, what motivates and demotivates her, what her personality is like, how she deals with stress, what her strengths are, what her weaknesses are, and how she will fit in with the rest of the team. And these only scratch the surface.

To outprepare your competition, you need to have positive, insightful answers to questions about yourself as a person—who you are as an individual. But this is not enough. Should your interviewer gloss over this important area, you must have, prepared and up your sleeve, a list of your most positive personal qualities and attributes, and you must be able to find a way to work them into the questions that you *are* asked. You can't risk waiting to be discovered; you've got to be in there selling yourself.

Your Career

We've already talked about your resume as a useful guide to your interview. You will get plenty of questions about why you did this, how you did that, why did you take this job, and why did you move to that job. Along these same lines, an astute interviewer will note that your resume details only the career choices that you actually made. She may ask about what other options you had, what paths you did not follow, what opportunities you missed, and what decisions you wish you could do over.

A good interviewer will not only want to learn about your career history, but he will want to know where you see your career going in the future. You should expect questions about your three-, five-, and perhaps 10-year goals, and how you see this job advancing your overall career plans.

This Job

You're not interviewing for just any job; you're interviewing for *this* job. Why do you want *this* job? It's a basic question, but you darn well better have a good answer for it. It is said that this single interview question from Roger Mudd torpedoed Ted Kennedy's quest for the U.S. presidency. You may not be running for political office, but I'd guess that this job you're interviewing for means more to your career and your family than anybody you'll ever vote for. A convincing response to why *this* job is the one for you will always stick in the interviewer's mind.

What have you learned about this job? Why is there an opening? What types of people succeed in this job? Who did it before? Where is she now? Is it a new position? What new opportunities does it represent? Your networking may have provided you with some of this information, the business press may have provided other information, and if you are working through a headhunter, she may be able to give you some insight. Hard though it may be, it is necessary to use all of your resources to gather pre-interview intelligence about the job for which you're interviewing.

This Company

When you go in for an interview, it is important that you demonstrate interest not only in the job, but also in the hiring organization. This type of preparation demonstrates to the interviewer that you are knowledgeable, thorough, and hardworking. A wealth of information is available about any organization. The key here is to allow yourself enough time before the interview to gather the information you need. You may be in the occasional situation in which, on the day before your interview, you are scrambling to build your data bank. Try to avoid this because, in your haste, you may miss an important piece of information. I hate to sound like your mom, but do your homework early and get it out of the way.

By this stage of your job hunt, you should be completely familiar with the sources of company information in your library or online, such as *Dun and Bradstreet's Million Dollar Directory, Standard & Poor's Register, Thomas Register,* and *Ward's Business Directory of U.S. Private Companies.* There are so many directories available that there is a "Directory of Directories." Combine these formal information sources with what you find in the business press, and on the Web, and what you have uncovered from your networking, and you will be able to develop a good picture of the company where you are interviewing.

Here are a few of the things you should know about your potential new employer *before* you go in for an interview:

✳ How it is owned: public or private.

✳ Size: number of employees, sales.

✳ Products, services.

✳ Financial health.

✳ Status in its industry.

✳ Legal problems, history, status in the community.

✳ Family-friendly rating.

✳ Organizational culture.

✳ Key staff.

✳ Typical pay scales and benefit packages.

This Industry

No organization exists in a vacuum. If you are interviewing for a job in a not-for-profit (NFP) organization, you need to understand the effect that 9/11 has had on fundraising across the entire NFP world. If you are interviewing for a job in a pharmaceutical company, you need to have some background knowledge about orphan drugs, the FDA approval process, and healthcare reform. Unless you are interviewing for one of the top jobs in the company, you don't have to be a bona fide expert on the industry, but you do need to be able to talk intelligently about the status of the industry, where it's headed, the current trends, the industry leaders, and so on.

Your reference librarian can help you uncover some of this information, but again I must stress that you must not leave this until the last minute. There are good sources of industry information out there, but not all of them are readily accessible. For example, finding the schedule of presentations from a recent industry trade show or convention, or tracking down a leading industry consultant to network with can take time.

And So On, and So On

We have progressed from having you prepared to talk about yourself, to being prepared to talk about the job you're interviewing for, about the company, and about the industry. We could continue ad infinitum to the economy, the country, the world, the universe, and the cosmos beyond. The point here is that the more generally informed you are about the world around you, the more interesting you are as a person, and the more interesting a job candidate you will be. You don't need to be a walking, talking almanac, but reading the daily newspaper and listening to the evening news can be a useful part of your overall interview preparation.

One of the ways for you to control the interview is not to see it as a big unknown. The unknown can translate into fear, fear can translate into stress, and stress can hurt your interview performance. Use Figure 4.1 on page 91 to help you think through your interview preparation. Your upcoming interview is *not* some big unknown. In fact, it is fairly predictable. Using this knowledge to thoroughly prepare will considerably reduce your fear, stress, and anxiety. You will have out-prepared your competition because every question you hear in your interview (even the ones that seem out of sequence or sound as if they're from left field) will fit somewhere into the interview plan you have meticulously constructed.

HOW TO ANSWER
A QUESTION

The title of this section sounds almost humorous, sort of like "how to drink water" or "how to breathe air." I mean, after all, you've been answering questions all of your life, right? But as with every other part of the job-hunting and interviewing process, I want you better informed and better prepared than your competition. There is a big difference between a good answer and an answer that makes them want to hire you *today*. There is a huge difference between the average job interview and a *winning* job interview. Having thought through precisely how you want to field the interviewer's question is essential to this process.

1. Listen actively to each question.

Watch your interviewer's body language and facial expressions—especially his eyes. It is perfectly acceptable to ask the interviewer to make something more clear or to restate the question. Naturally, you don't want to do this after each question, but it is critical for you to know what the interviewer is trying to learn about you. Other forms of active listening that can help you here are paraphrasing or restating the question to confirm that you're both on the same wavelength.

2. Take a second or two to frame your answer.

You're not a gumball machine that the interviewer pops a quarter into, and immediately out pops an answer. If you respond too quickly, it will sound as if you're over-programmed and not really thinking about your answers. (Of course, on the other side of the coin, if you respond too slowly, it may appear that you have drifted off to La-La Land.) You may have a great answer prepared and ready to go, but take a moment to understand what it is she's going for. (We'll deal with stupid questions later, but sometimes this process—looking for the rationale behind a question—can help you generate a stronger response.)

3. Never let them put negative words in your mouth.

Using negative words makes you sound negative; using positive words makes you sound positive. This is a technique politicians have long known. Stay positive. Your last company wasn't the "hell-hole" it was portrayed as in the press; it was "full of challenges that helped me learn to deal productively with conflict." Your last boss wasn't a "mean S.O.B.," he was "demanding, but with a style very different from my own." Which brings us to my next point.

4. Always tell the truth.

Of course, it's the right thing to do morally, but also, the truth always makes the best answer because it looks and sounds like, well, the truth.

Quick quiz: What's the opposite of dishonesty? Most folks answer *honesty*, and most folks are wrong. A quick look at Figure 4.2 (Dr. Paul's

Figure 4.2

Dr. Paul's Guide to Honesty and Survival

Dishonesty: "My boss was great."
Honesty: "My boss was tough but I can work with all types."
Brutal Honesty: "My boss was a tyrannical idiot."

Guide to Honesty and Survival) on this page demonstrates that the polar opposite of dishonesty is brutal honesty—honesty without common sense, honesty without compassion. People who have managed to stay married for a while usually have this figured out. Consider the question, "How was dinner?" Which is the better answer: (a) "I wouldn't feed it to the dog!" or (b) "Interesting, but it can't compare to your famous chicken Marsala"? Obviously, the answer is b. This may sound a little weasel-like, but you haven't been dishonest, you haven't hurt anybody's feelings, and you're not wearing something you wouldn't, in fact, feed to the dog.

Staying positive while staying truthful will mean that you have to carefully couch some of your answers. Intelligent interviewers will know you are doing this, may try to explore the issue a little more, and will respect your savvy in staying positive. Remember: every potential employer sees himself as your potential ex-employer, and you will increase their comfort level with you by demonstrating tact and professionalism.

5. A minute or two is enough.

Don't drone on and on. This is a big mistake many folks make when answering some of those open-ended questions, such as "Tell me about yourself." If the interviewer wants to get into something in great detail, she will ask another question.

THE SOUNDS
OF SILENCE

Try this experiment: While talking to a friend, suddenly stop talking, stay silent for four or five seconds (check your watch for accuracy), and then start talking again. Your friend may ask you if you dozed off or were having a heart attack or something. What this little experiment shows is how noticeable even a tiny bit of silence is.

When you are under some stress, this little bit of time may seem exaggerated. Thus, the few seconds it takes you to frame an answer or the time it takes an interviewer to ask the next question may seem overly long. Don't read too much into this, and don't worry about this—it's normal.

Psychotherapists have long understood the power of silence to get someone to open up. Some interviewers will use this technique on you. But you don't need to fill every second of air time. Don't fidget or start adjusting your clothes.

If you have fully answered the last question, simply sit there quietly, take a couple of relaxing deep breaths, and await the next question. If you have stumbled onto the dreaded idiot interviewer who thinks he can stress you out by staring at you, calmly return his gaze with a welcoming, anticipating look on your face.

Other interviewers may simply be struggling to find another good question to ask you. As we discussed earlier, many interviewers are not especially well trained and try to take great care not to look foolish or say something stupid or ask something that could be illegal. (In fact, many interviewers hate interviewing and are more uncomfortable than the person they are interviewing.) If you judge this to be the situation (after 15 seconds or so), mention that you have some questions that you would like to ask and see if this is an appropriate time to do so. If your interviewer is floundering, your offer will come as a godsend.

ASK AND YOU
SHALL RECEIVE

In the last chapter we discussed the way you should look at the interview as a two-way street. Obviously, they are interviewing you, but, in reality, you are also interviewing them. You hope they will be offering you money for your work, but you are offering them weeks, months, and years of your life. What's more valuable, in your book?

Because most good interviewers will ask you, at some point, if you have any questions, you need to have prepared some good ones. Even if the interviewer doesn't ask you if you have questions, I want you to have some good ones prepared so that you can try to ask them. This happens most frequently toward the end of the interview.

The best questions you can ask in the interview can accomplish two things. They can transmit positive information about you to the interviewer, and they can get you data to help you decide if this is the place you want to work. Let's take them in turn.

Giving Data

You want your interviewer to assess you positively. You want her to know that you have done your homework and that you are very interested in this position and in this organization. Questions to help you accomplish these goals should be based on the research work you have already done. Some examples are:

＊ "I read in your annual report that this company is rapidly expanding in Latin America. My Spanish is only fair to middling, but I'm interested in becoming more fluent. Does the training department offer courses in this area?" This question demonstrates three things: (1) you have done some homework on the company, (2) you have some tools that could be useful in a growth area of the company, and (3) you are interested in continuing to develop your skills.

＊ "I remember reading in the paper last year that St. Vitus Hospital merged with two other hospitals, one larger and one smaller. We went through something similar a few years back at Mercy General. I'm curious as to how the staff handled it—has the culture changed significantly?" This question demonstrates three things: (1) you are knowledgeable about the hospital and the industry, (2) you have some experience that is directly relevant to what this hospital may be going through, and (3) you are interested in the insight and observations of the interviewer.

Getting Data

If you are fortunate enough to get a job offer, what else do you need to know about this organization before you would accept it? Let this issue help you to construct some other useful questions to ask in your interview. We will talk about money later, but beyond financial considerations, you want to be confident that you can succeed in the job, right? So use this golden opportunity to clarify as many issues as you can. Some examples are:

＊ "Can you show me an organizational chart? Because we're talking about a supervisory job in order management, I'm interested in how the group's relationship between sales and customer service is structured. Who are the managers of those groups? How do they interact? How do they get along?" These questions show that you are already identifying with the goals of your potential new department, that you are savvy enough to predict friction between certain groups, and that you will probably work proactively to sort out these types of issues early in your tenure.

✳ "Elroy, you've worked in this organization for a while. How would you describe the culture? What types of people seem to really succeed here?" This question demonstrates that you are interested in your interviewer's perceptions and opinions, it helps you get some inside information about the organization, and it may give you a shopping list of personal traits or characteristics that they are looking for in a new hire.

You will not get a huge amount of time to ask questions during your job interviews, so make each one count. Tool #7 in the Toolkit, Preparing Winning Questions to Ask in Your Interview, gives you a systematic method for generating some great questions. If you use this form to help you further prepare for your interview, you will be able to strengthen your candidacy for this job, gather data you might not be able to access in any other way, and possibly pick up subtle messages from the interviewer that he may not even know he is sending (for example, how many other candidates are in the loop and the degree of interest they have in hiring you). Last, but not least, you are giving the interviewer time to talk, and because most people prefer talking to listening, this will ultimately work in your favor.

HOW DO YOU GET TO
CARNEGIE HALL?

Don't tell me that you've never heard the joke that's as old as the hills. A little girl walking down a New York City street stops a wise old man and asks, "How do you get to Carnegie Hall?" He pauses, thinks, and says, "Practice, practice, practice."

There are only so many times in your career when you will be actively out job hunting. A process you engage in only occasionally throughout the period of a couple of decades isn't anything in which you will automatically develop a whole lot of proficiency. Add to this the relatively low number of bona fide interviews you will get during any active job search. What we end up with is a fairly rare, irregularly occurring task at which you want to be at peak performance levels. This is a completely unrealistic expectation unless you get plenty of structured practice.

Some job hunters practice their interviewing skills during their first few interviews. Unfortunately, often these first few interviews are with the organizations that job hunters most want to work in. This results in using these critical skills at their lowest peak with their prime job targets. Bad strategy, bad tactics.

Before you ever walk into your first real job interview, I want you to have spent a minimum of four to six hours practicing your interviewing skills. Some job hunters have told me that this is excessive. Horse hockey! Your interviewing skills must be primed at the outset. The first position you interview for during this campaign could be the best one you encounter during the entire job hunt. This may seem excessively lucky to you, but luck is what happens to the well prepared.

Solo Practice

The first part of practicing your interview skills should be done alone. Spend all the time you need on Tool #6 and Tool #7 in the Toolkit (Frequently Asked Interview Questions and Preparing Winning Questions to Ask in Your Interview). Compile a list of the questions that will be hardest for you to answer. With this list in front of you, ask yourself each question out loud. Yes, *each* question, and, yes, *out loud*. Then answer the question out loud. How does it sound? Where is it weak? How can it be improved? Does the answer demonstrate something about your personal characteristics, your knowledge, and your experience? Answer it again and again until it sounds solid, believable, and positive.

When you feel you have a good answer, note the number of the question in a spiral-bound notebook, and beside the question write down a few words or phrases that will bring your answer to mind. (As time permits, eventually work your way through all 107 questions.) Do not write out the entire text of the answer. You will be reviewing these notes later and you don't want to risk memorizing complete sentences that will make you sound like a tape recorder. Working your way through the list will take a good amount of time, so start now. Many job hunters want to skip this step. However, I can't stress strongly enough that landing a job you can love for months and years of your life is darn well worth a few hours of work now.

Mock Interviews

For the second part of your interview practice program you will need a partner or two. This partner could be a spouse, a close friend, a counselor, a coach, or someone from your job-search support group. I suggest you use someone who is also currently job hunting because you can learn from each other's efforts.

Make a copy of the Mock Interview Preparation Tool (#8 in the Toolkit). Fill in items 1 through 7 and then give it to your practice interviewer to add her questions to item 8. Now you have a script for your mock interview.

One way that you can quickly and dramatically improve your interviewing skills is to videotape your mock interviews and review them later with your interviewer. This, again, is something most job hunters resist. Unless you are often mistaken for people such as Jennifer Lopez or Brad Pitt, you are not going to be happy with the way you look on videotape. (I'll bet even J.Lo and Brad nitpick their appearance.) Get over it! What we're looking for, among other things, is how you come across to the interviewer, how you handle the questions, how you deal with the transition from answering questions to asking questions, and your overall personal presentation.

Today's video cameras are easy to use; if you don't own one, borrow one from a friend. Many of today's cell phones have a video feature. Set it up on a bookcase or table so that it focuses solely on you, the job hunter. (This isn't *60 Minutes*. We don't care how the interviewer comes across.) Your interviewer should be someone who understands that, although this may be a bit fun, it is important practice and serious business. (This is another good reason to recruit another job hunter for this job.) Once the camera is set and checked, start it, reenter the room as you would for an interview, and, with your partner using your script, role-play your interview for 50 to 60 minutes. If you make a mistake or make a misstatement, do not start over. Learning to come back from a bumble or a stumble is a valuable part of the process.

After your mock interview, do not review the tape alone; you will be far too critical of yourself. Do it with someone else, preferably your interview partner, who can tell you what it was like at the moment. Using the Mock Interview Evaluation Tool (#9 in the Toolkit), evaluate yourself as if you were evaluating someone else. Be as dispassionate and objective as you can. The idea is neither to beat yourself up nor give yourself an automatic pat on the back. Your goal is to get feedback you can use to improve your next interview. Incorporate this information into your next mock interview and continue this process until your interviewing skills are honed to a razor's edge.

In the Mock Interview Evaluation Tool you'll notice a few questions about uncovering objections and using a strong close. These are professional sales techniques refined by generations of successful salespeople. Understood and used properly, they will help you separate yourself from other merely good interviewers and distinguish yourself as a truly *winning* job interviewer. They deserve some significant attention and focus of their own, so we'll devote Chapter 6 entirely to how to close the deal and get the job offer. But before we even think of closing the interview, an often overlooked but invaluable job-interviewing resource needs your attention: your job references.

CHAPTER 5

HOW TO HAVE GLOWING JOB REFERENCES

There is an essential tool that is too often given short shrift by job hunters. It is your set of job references. Some job hunters ask for a supervisor or two to be a reference and sit back, hoping they will say something positive. Others wait until they are asked for references at the end of an interview before they give them much thought. Both approaches are dead wrong because:

1. Despite a person's best intentions, you never know what someone will say about you until you have at least discussed it with him or her.

2. The time to prepare your references is now—before you get out there interviewing—when you have the time and clarity of mind to think who can best help you in this vital role and how best they can do it.

WHY
BOTHER?

The best reason for you to invest the time and energy to prepare a glowing set of references is because, most of the time, your references will be checked only if you are a bona fide finalist for the position. You will have worked your heart out to get to this point in the process, and there may well be only one more step between you and success. Sometimes references will be checked on a couple of finalists, but most often I hear employers say something such as, "If his references check out, let's make him an offer." This is where, as the old saying goes, there is often a slip between cup and lip.

Although I'm willing to admit that not all interviewers will ask you for your references, they will be requested more frequently as you move into ever more responsible positions in your career. I've seen estimates that references are not checked somewhere between 25 to 50 percent of the time. Different reasons are given for these low numbers. One is the perception that former employers are reluctant to say anything negative that could result in a lawsuit. Another is that some former employers are wary of unwittingly omitting a piece of data that could get them sued by the new employer. (Both of these reasons are the result of the fact that we have more lawyers in this country than fruit flies.) One reason *I've* frequently seen is that some interviewers trust their own gut instincts more than they do data from an unknown party. Though interesting, this information should have no effect on you.

The fact that some interviewers will not be checking your references is just further proof that you are better educated about the hiring process than they are. The fact that some interviewers will check your references means that you must have them well prepared for *all* interviewers.

WHEN: TWO

TIMING TIPS

No, this is not a section on how to get away with running around behind your significant other's back. That's what daytime television is for, and as a dedicated job hunter and winning job interviewer, you are forbidden to watch daytime TV. What we're talking about here are the two critical points in the job reference process: when to prepare them and when to offer them.

Now, now, now. *That's* when you have to start prepping your references. Even if you're not sure when your next job hunt will begin, start prepping your references now. Think about your job references as though they were valuable tools in your toolbox; you need to take them out and inspect them every once in a while just to make sure they're in good shape for when you're going to need them next. And if you're currently in the job hunt, you don't have a minute to lose.

You need to start prepping your references now, before you're asked to provide them, for a couple of reasons. Unless you are a *Jeopardy!* champion, you're probably not at your best when trying desperately to retrieve important facts from your brain while attempting to smile casually like James Bond when, in fact, you feel more like Homer Simpson watching the nuclear plant melt down. As I mentioned earlier, this is an important step in the interview process, so I don't recommend you try to dredge stuff up on the spur of the moment. *D'oh!*

Adequately preparing your job references takes time, and once you're asked for them, *ding*, the bell rings and you're out of time, but thanks for playing, better luck next time. You need time to think of who you want as references, you need to think about how you're going to ask them, you may need time to track them down if some are from one or two jobs ago, you need time to call them, you need time for them to call you back, and you need time to meet with them, preferably face to face. Oh, and multiply this amount of time by the number of references you need to prepare. (I suggest four to six as a minimum.) In fact, don't start now; start yesterday.

There is one last reason for you to start prepping your references early in the job hunt: Unless you are seriously masochistic, you will be using references who have positive things to say about you. Because these people already think highly of you (and you'll soon be reminding them of just *how* highly), why not ask for their assistance early in your job hunt? These people are a unique part of your contact network. Tap their expertise the way you would any network contact. Ask them what sources of published openings they know of. What online resources or career Websites are they aware of? Do they know of or have access to an especially great library? Do they have any human resources contacts, or can they personally refer you to an employment recruiter? Do they have any potential job leads or any other creative job-hunting resources for you? Will they give you other names for your network? And, of course, are they willing to be contacted as a reference for you?

Should all professional and conscientious hiring managers check references? Absolutely. Should all professional and conscientious job candidates have a well-prepared set of job references? Absolutely. If your interviewer doesn't ask for your references, should you offer them? Absolutely *not*. Take a quick look back at Figure 2.1 on page 61. I want this to remind you that checking references is one more step between you and the job offer you want. Just because you have a great set of references all prepared and ready to go does *not* mean you need to give them. The answer to the question, "When do I give my references?" is: *only after there is a strong mutual desire to move forward, and only when you are asked for them.*

If you are not going to actively pursue the position in question, do not offer your references. Why would you bother these people who are willing to go out of their way to help you when you don't really need their help? Your references are valuable resources, so keep them in reserve for when you actually need them. To the latter point, if an organization wants to hire you without running you (and your references) through another step in this long and hard process, bully for you. For goodness sake, don't remind them that there's another potential hurdle for you to jump; that's their problem, not yours.

WHOM

TO USE

Whom you want to use for references depends, to some degree, on what type of job you're hunting for. The most frequently requested job reference is your most recent boss. If you are currently employed and your boss doesn't know you're job hunting, this presents a bit of a problem. My advice would be to offer your previous boss. If the interviewer still wants to talk to your current boss, remember that Dr. Paul has advised you that you are under no obligation to commit career suicide. There are ways around this, however.

You may belong to that fortunate minority who has a boss who wants you to succeed in your career and realizes that, sometimes, for that to happen, people have to move on. If you can trust your boss not to penalize you for job hunting, you know it right at the moment you are reading this. Good for you. Have a heart-to-heart talk with your boss and prepare him the way you would any other reference. If you are at all uncertain about it, don't risk blowing your cover. Tell your interviewer that you will be happy to provide all of your references, including your current boss, with the understanding that references from your current organization will be checked only after you have an offer in hand (that is written) and an agreed-upon start date, and that you will have the opportunity to give your current employer adequate notice of your resignation. If your potential new employer is not willing to treat you professionally and with respect and does not value your desire to make a career transition in a civil and dignified manner by not leaving your employer in a lurch, well, what does that tell you? Maybe this isn't your dream job after all. Sorry 'bout that, but it's better to know that now, before the fact.

You should have two (and preferably three) former bosses prepared to use as references. If you have supervised or managed other people, you should also have a couple of key former subordinates on your reference list. If you have or have had responsibilities for managing relationships outside of your employing organization (for example, vendors, suppliers, contractors, consultants, and volunteers), you should have a few of them prepared as well. Do not use people such as your clergyperson, your accountant, your best friend, or your neighbor. These are personal references and are more appropriate for a rental or mortgage application, social organization, or motorcycle gang.

HOW TO
PREPARE THEM

You have now decided whom you should be using for references: articulate, positive, helpful people who can speak cogently about your knowledge, experience, work habits, and interpersonal skills. Once you have compiled your list of potential references, start calling them.

The purpose of this call is to renew your acquaintance (chitchat about people you know in common, update family matters, and so on), bring them up to date on your job hunt, and ask for a meeting to discuss your reference. Period. The purpose of the call is *not* to prepare your reference. Can't you do this by phone? Sure, I guess you can do it by smoke signals if you want to, but meeting in person is the best way of securing the most positive reference possible. Your job is to have glowing—not merely good—references, and the way to do this is to outprepare your competition. Of course, if this person is on the other side of the country or abroad, it will not be possible. But don't take the lazy approach if your references are local.

When you meet for coffee, breakfast, or lunch, take a copy of the Job Reference Data Form (#11 in the Toolkit) with you. This is actually a reference preparation tool, but because they will probably see it as you take notes, you don't want them to see "preparation" and think you're trying to put words in their mouth (which, in fact, is precisely what you are trying to do). Ask if she can offer you some ideas or tips about your job search and let her advise you. (Everybody likes to be asked for advice.) Then, pop the question, "So, Paul, would you be willing to serve as a reference for me?" or something like that. But ask the question directly. If they have reservations, it's better for you to know it now.

Start filling out the form as you are talking and make sure to find out how and where they prefer to be contacted—at home, at work, cell phone, private line, or what. Refresh your reference's memory as to how long you've known each other and in what roles and in what organizations. On pages 112–113 you will find a list of many of the reference questions I have heard throughout the last 20 years. Pick the ones you feel are most appropriate to the position you are looking for and discus them with your reference. The reason for doing this is to expand the reference data beyond the generic "he's great" or "he's terrific" comments that won't do you much good. You want to help your reference remember all the great things you did together, all the successes you had, how you dealt with setbacks, and, yes, what a great person you are. This means, of course, that you will have already spent some time resurrecting these memories yourself. Be sure to discuss your strengths and weaknesses and be ready to suggest some with which you are comfortable. Another reference question that's almost guaranteed to be asked is why you left the job your reference is discussing. Ask who else he might offer as a reference if the interviewer asks for someone else to talk to. (To help prevent this process from going too far afield, it's wise to have two people prepared to suggest each other.) Continue to make notes during this conversation so, later, you can recall who will be saying what. When your meeting is over, remember to thank your reference and indicate that you will do your best to give him a heads-up call prior to being contacted. This is an obvious courtesy, but it also gives you the chance to help fine-tune the reference with your input about the interviewer, the company, and the specific job in question.

When you go home or get back to the office, immediately send a note thanking your reference for his advice, support, and willingness to serve as a reference. Include a copy of your updated resume and a copy of the Job Reference Data Form that you just completed. This gives your reference plenty of data to draw upon when called, and it helps reinforce the message that you are an appreciative, thoughtful, and well-organized professional. Now you can add this person's name and contact information to your reference list. (See Sample Job Reference Listing Sheet, Tool #12 in the Toolkit.)

SAMPLE REFERENCE
QUESTIONS

* How long have you known him? In what roles?
* What was his salary?
* How would you describe his personality?
* What are his strengths? Weaknesses? Can you give me a situation in which you observed them?
* What was the quality of his work?
* What are his work habits?
* Why did he leave the company?
* Would you hire him back if you could?
* Did he require a lot of supervision? How independent is he?
* How much responsibility did he have?
* Do you know if he has ever been fired?
* What would his peers and subordinates tell me about him?
* Can you give me an example of how he learned from an error he made?
* How does he handle conflict?
* What frustrates him?
* How does he handle pressure and deadlines?
* What could he have done to improve his performance?
* Do you think this job fits in with his long-range career plans? Why?
* What would be the ideal role for her?
* What motivates him?
* What turns him off?

* Given the scope of this job, what kind of a fit do you see here?
* Can you think of anything else that would help me get a more rounded picture of him?
* Who else would be a good person for me to talk to about him?

REFERENCE
GLITCHES

As with everything else in job hunting, you might run into a few potential potholes in the reference process. Not to worry—there are ways you can deal with all of them. The important thing is not to panic. Stay cool, and work your way around them.

The "No Reference" Policy

Some organizations have a "no reference" policy. They may only provide dates of employment, job title, and salary. If you run into this, you can ask your reference if she would be willing to give you a *personal* reference. (If she won't, she won't. There's nothing else you can do. Move on to someone else.) However, you are asking people who think highly of you to help you, and most of them will. Be sure to double-check where and how they prefer to be contacted.

It is perfectly appropriate to inform your interviewer that this particular employer has a "no reference" policy and that you have asked for a personal reference. Most hiring managers have run into this before and know how to gently tread in this area, because if they come on too strong, they get little or no additional information.

The Negative Reference

There two types of negative references. One is the person whom you prepared and who indicated that he would say great things about you, and then rips you up behind your back. If you have taken the time to prepare your references, this probably won't happen because you can usually see in someone's eyes if he is being genuine with you. This goes to the point that even though you prepared a reference, you still may not want to use him. It is up to you to determine if the person, in fact, will be a good reference for you. But on a rare occasion, you might get sandbagged. You'll only find out about this if the interviewer shares it with you. Obviously, you'll never offer this person as a reference again, but right now you need a response.

I suggest that you express your honest surprise and then say something such as "I hope the fact that this person would say great things to my face and then turn around and say negative things behind my back says more about him than me. In any event, I would be pleased to have you speak with someone else who can comment on my performance in that job and see how they viewed me." And then offer another reference. (This is why you can never have too many prepared.) This is damage control, but it's the best you can do. Forget about this loser. He will be coming back in his next life as a dung beetle. Remember: time not only heals all wounds, it also wounds all heels.

The other negative reference is someone (such as a former boss) who is well known, who may be called as a reference regardless of whether you supply her name, and who may not be one of your strongest supporters. In fact, maybe she fired you. If this is the case, I still want you to make an effort to prepare her as a reference. Time may have softened her opinion of you. She may now recognize the difficult position that you were in at the time. At the very least, ask her to give a balanced picture of your contributions if she is contacted. Obviously, don't offer this person as a reference if you can help it, and, if you have to, always pair her with another reference who is familiar with whatever the situation was and who will give it a more positive perspective.

Missing in Action

"I can't find my old boss." "I can't remember that VP's name." "That job was years ago; who would be interested now?" "That company has been bought and sold twice since I was there. Nobody's left that would remember me." I hear this stuff a lot. I try to be supportive, but I really just want to say, "Boo-hoo! You've misplaced your references! Now stop whining, get to work, and go find them."

These are *your* references. You've worked long and hard for them. You've earned them. They are an invaluable interviewing resource. I don't have time now to beat you up about not having maintained them the way you were supposed to. You need to invest some time tracking them down; use your other contacts, former colleagues, phone books, old Rolodex, professional associations, trade groups, alumni associations, and, of course, the Web and your social networking sites. Once you have rebuilt your reference list, never let it get out of date again. Think of excuses (Christmas, birthdays, Groundhog Day) to stay in touch. You will need your job references for as long as you are in the working world, so give them the time and energy they deserve.

CLOSING
THE LOOP

You've thoroughly prepared a solid reference list, you've offered it to the interviewer (but only when asked), you've alerted your references as to who will be calling, and you've told them a little about why you are perfect for the job. The sum total of your interviewing and job references may get you the job offer you want. Or the job opening may be put on hold, or they might promote from within, or they may hire someone else from the outside, or they may reopen the search. Or, or, or. Regardless of what happens, at this point, get another note out to your references thanking them for taking the time to speak with the interviewer on your behalf. Again, this is only common courtesy, but it also keeps your support team involved, informed, and motivated to keep helping you.

THREE LAST
THINGS

I have three final pieces of advice for you regarding your job references.

Letters of Recommendation

In the era before phone, fax, and e-mail, letters of recommendation were commonly used. This is not the case today. In our increasingly litigious society, nobody wants to put anything negative down on paper about someone else, so any letters are uniformly positive and usually dismissed as fluff. You will still see job advertisements in education and some scientific journals requesting them, and first-time job hunters still use them. But for anything other than an entry-level job, your interviewer will want to speak to some live human beings.

As with most rules, there are exceptions. If one of your references will be incommunicado during a significant part of your job hunt (on the international space station or paddling up the Congo in a dugout canoe, for example), then you may want to secure a letter of recommendation. But otherwise, don't bother.

Security Clearances

If you are being interviewed for a sensitive government job, for a defense contractor, or for a position in homeland security, you will probably be screened for security clearance. Whereas your job references focus on your job performance, a security clearance investigation includes a lot of other stuff, such as fingerprinting, verifying all your old addresses and your foreign travel, talking to current and former neighbors, and, generally, compiling a complete file on where you've been and what you've done for your whole life.

If this is the sort of job you want, this is a process with which you've got to come to terms. I rather like the idea of scary men with big guns asking the neighbors about me; it creates just the mystique I'm going for. But if you want to keep a low profile with the government (as if you could), then positions in these fields may not be for you.

Credit Checks

It seems as if we're getting pretty far afield from job references, but we're not. Many organizations hiring a senior executive will conduct a credit check along with checking job references to get a handle on how this person manages his own affairs. In the United States you can check your credit rating with the major credit rating agencies for free once a year. Even if this is not the case where you live, fiscal prudence in the era of identity theft suggests that you should do so anyway.

I know this chapter has outlined a more comprehensive reference preparation regimen than you are probably used to. I know it involves a lot of work. I also know it will help you stand head and shoulders above your competition—and make no mistake about it: there are other job hunters out there who are competing with you for the job you want. My question to you is this: Do you want this job badly enough to do what it takes to win it? If you do, then you are well on your way—with a pocketful of glowing references—to a job you can love.

The issue of job references will only arise after a level of interest is expressed—usually toward the end of the interview. It's important not to let the interview end on this tentative "let's wait and see what the references have to say" note. Successful salespeople—those who make a fabulous living by selling goods or services to other people—know that how a meeting, a sales call, or a job interview concludes has a powerful effect on the ultimate result. In Chapter 6 you will learn the techniques of the successful salesperson that you need in order to successfully close your winning job interviews.

CHAPTER 6

HOW TO CLOSE THE DEAL AND GET THE JOB OFFER

The professional job search requires many skills: self-assessment skills, research skills, organizational skills, telephone skills, administrative skills, marketing skills, and, right at the top of the list, sales skills. However, most people in the world of work are *not* salespeople. (This is another reason most people hate job hunting.) The statistical likelihood is that you are not a salesperson. Don't worry about this; salespeople are created, not born. Plus, you don't have any bad habits to unlearn. If you *are* a salesperson, I don't need to remind you that many of the people who are in sales are not very good at it. (This is one of the reasons that salespeople are sometimes held in such low regard.) Even if you are in the top 1 percent of super salespeople, this chapter will help you incorporate your superior sales skills into the winning job interview. In this chapter I will explain how the ordinary job hunter can use the secrets of the super salesperson to convert a higher percentage of those hard-won job interviews into bona fide job offers.

SALES
MYTHS

There are many misconceptions about professional selling. One is that the sale is a contest of wills—one in which the salesperson keeps talking and talking so that she wears down a resistant buyer until, ultimately, they both collapse in an exhausted heap over a completed deal. Nothing could be further from the truth. Any professional sale of goods or services should be a meeting of the minds, a meeting where the salesperson learns the needs and desires of the buyer and where the buyer learns how the product or service the seller is offering can help meet her needs and desires. If the salesperson is not actively listening for the potential buyer's needs, the sale will not happen. If the salesperson is preaching ("my product is great") rather than teaching ("here's why my product is great"), the sale will not happen. These two points reinforce why the winning job interview must be an exchange of ideas, not a one-way infomercial.

Another sales myth is that there is only one successful sales personality. The stereotypical image of the successful salesperson is that of a sharply dressed, fast-talking extrovert. Although some personality types do have an easier time learning professional sales techniques, many low-key, informal introverts make excellent salespeople. (Warren Buffett, investor extraordinaire, and Bill Gates, who built the biggest software company in the world, come to mind.) Regardless of what type of personality you have, you can learn and easily use super sales techniques to your enormous advantage.

The last sales myth I'll touch on here is that some things sell themselves. What hooey. Every product or service must be fully and engagingly described to the potential buyer in a way that demonstrates how it meets the buyer's needs and desires. You couldn't sell chocolate-covered bars of gold bullion for 10 cents a pound unless you knew how to fit their desirable characteristics to the needs and desires of the customer, and then (drum roll, please) help your buyer overcome whatever objections, logical or illogical, he may have so that you can close the deal.

WHAT IS
A "CLOSE"?

In the terms of professional sales training, the "close" is when you strive to uncover any objections or reservations your potential customer has, and you help your potential customer communicate the decision she has made during your presentation. Notice I said *help* your potential customer, not intimidate, dominate, or bludgeon. An intelligent potential buyer (that is, your interviewer) will resist any effort by you to manipulate or overwhelm him *even if* he has already made a potential buying decision in your favor.

There are those few occasions when some buyers can be bullied or mesmerized into putting their name on the dotted line or saying yes, but getting them to follow through (that is, putting through the purchase order or taking delivery) will be next to impossible. They were probably just agreeing with you to get you out of their office.

A close is successful if the buyer immediately responds and says, "Yes, I love what you're selling; when can it be delivered?" Interestingly, the close is also successful if it succeeds in uncovering an objection that the buyer has to the sale. Only by discovering potential objections can the salesperson tailor her presentation to more fully explain how her product or service can meet the needs and desires of the potential buyer. If those objections exist but remain unspoken, they cannot be overturned; the sale will not happen, and, even worse, the salesperson will never know why.

YOU MEAN I *WANT*
OBJECTIONS?

In a word, yup. Your job interview is a sales call in which you communicate your knowledge, skills, experience, and personal qualities in an effort to demonstrate that you meet, and, you hope, even exceed the needs and desires of the potential buyer. Through your pre-interview research and by asking insightful interview questions, you have uncovered these needs (the job specifications). Via your interview answers you have succinctly but completely presented the reasons why you can do the job in question. Now you need to *help your potential customer express the decision he has made during your presentation.*

THE TRIAL
CLOSE

The trial close is when you ask a question to get a feeling for how ready your buyer is to make a decision. After you have answered a question about some aspect of your background that closely relates to the job you're interviewing for, an effective trial close might be, "Dr. Scruton, I'm really glad you asked me about my dog training experience. When I was thinking about this interview I was hoping you'd agree that such experience would be a great asset to someone working in your animal clinic." Notice this is one of those "non-question questions." You're not "forcing" him to respond, but if he does there are three potential outcomes:

1. Dr. Scruton agrees with you and tells you that he is ready to hire you. This is the best news. You can stop selling and start working out the details.

2. Dr. Scruton agrees with you and asks another question. This is also good news in that he has bought one of your selling points and is now moving on to discover more.

3. Dr. Scruton disagrees with you. But how you handle this disagreement—this objection—can still provide you with a selling opportunity.

Let's look at another example of a trial close. It's nearing the end of your interview. You've been asked a lot of questions, and you've asked a couple of good ones yourself. Try something like this: "Mr. Castleman, I realize our time is starting to get short. I've really enjoyed learning more about Southern Beverages and I think I could be very successful here. (Pause a moment here to look for some nonverbal feedback.) What questions or issues have I left unanswered?"

Notice a few things that are built into this trial close. You have shown appropriate courtesy, which is always a good idea. (I don't call it "common courtesy" because, these days, it's not so common.) You have expressed strong interest in the job and have given your positive evaluation of the fit between your background and the needs of the job. You're not blaming Mr. Castleman for not having asked enough questions; you're accepting that *you* might have left something unsaid. You have left Mr. Castleman with an opportunity to endorse your candidacy and suggest a positive next step. And most importantly, if Mr. Castleman has a reservation about your candidacy, you have offered him the opportunity to get it out in the open so that you can address it, or, even better, overturn it.

Very few job hunters can think up great trial closes on the spur of the moment such as the ones presented here. This is why Tools #9, #10, and #13 in the Toolkit all have sections to help you prepare, practice, and evaluate how you can close your interviews on the strongest note possible.

When Do You Use a Trial Close?

There are three answers to this question. The trial close used in the interview with Dr. Scruton at the Scruton Animal Clinic example demonstrates an old sales axiom that you can remember with the letters A-B-C (Always Be Closing). In job interviewing this works only after some level of mutual interest is established. Come on too strong, too early, and it won't work. But after you're well into the interview and if you have a strong feeling that it's going well, you might slip in one of those "non-question questions" and see how you're really doing.

The traditional time to try a trial close in the job interview is demonstrated in the Southern Beverages example. Working it in near the end of the interview has a more natural feel to it, but it comes with a risk. Your interviewer may indicate more than one possible objection. This is not necessarily a deal-breaker, but if you have only another five or 10 minutes left in the interview, you may not have time to address them all. This is why it's usually a good strategy to try to slip in a subtle trial close when you estimate that you have at least 25 percent of your interview time remaining.

In my consulting practice I've had the opportunity to learn from a number of super-successful salespeople. More than a few have told me that there is no single best time to try to close a sale. What they suggest is to always be on the lookout for a buying signal. At whatever point they see or hear a buying signal, they will use a trial close to solidify the progress they've made up to that point and to see if the potential buyer has made up his mind.

BUYING
SIGNALS

Interviewers transmit two kinds of buying signals: overt and covert. The winning job interviewer will pick up on both and seize the opportunity for a trial close. The *overt* buying signals are the ones we love to hear and are easy to pick up on. They include:

* "You sound like our kind of person."
* "That (specific experience or skill) would be quite useful to us."
* "What kind of notice would you have to give your current employer?"
* "I think you'll fit right in."
* "When can you start?"

It's important to stay focused and remember that you still have to close the interview on the strongest possible note. Despite the very positive impression these buying signals may give you, nobody has yet said, "You're hired!"

Covert buying signals from the interviewer are a lot more subtle and may only be well-prepared questions designed to dig below the surface of your candidacy. This is good news because it shows a growing level of interest in you. After hearing a few of these signals, you should work in a trial close. Some samples of *covert* buying signals are:

* "That's a good approach. How do you think it would work here?"

✳ "I love that story. That stuff happens here all the time."

✳ "That makes sense on the supplier side, but tell me how it would work on the user side."

✳ "How would you recommend that we restructure that department?"

✳ "Your approach makes sense to me."

HERE'S HOW
TO DO IT

You've picked up on a buying signal or two, you've tried a trial close, and (surprise surprise) you've uncovered an objection. This is a good thing. Your interviewer had an objection and you succeeded in uncovering it. That was your goal. Don't get defensive, because if you do, you won't be able to truly understand the point your interviewer is trying to make. And if you don't fully understand her point, you won't be able to deal with it effectively.

What is helpful to understand here is how the job specification or description was compiled in the first place. Human resources professionals tell me that very few job descriptions are real works of art. Although some may be accurate descriptions of the job to be filled, others may just be a list of the duties of the person who last had the job. It may be a supervisor's wish list describing a virtual super-person, or it may be a minimal bare-bones list suitable for a newspaper ad. It's going to be darn hard to get a candidate that is an exact fit to a job spec that, itself, is far from precise. Some candidates will be stronger in one area than another. Some candidates will bring attractive and much-needed skills that don't even appear in the job description. In short, one of the reasons *you* are not the perfect job candidate for a particular job is because there probably are *no* perfect job candidates for any particular job.

Another important point to remember is that the purpose of this interview is to get a job offer, *not* to win you a debating trophy.

An objection is a detour, not a roadblock. You don't need to change the interviewer's mind on every single point any more than you need to fix every pothole you find in the road. The interviewer is a human being whose observations are as worthy of respect as yours are. Treating his objection respectfully communicates your professionalism and your objectivity.

The objection you've uncovered doesn't necessarily mean that you won't get the job. In fact, how you handle the objection may well account for your landing the job.

TO OVERTURN OR ADDRESS
AN OBJECTION

Let's go back to the Southern Beverages example. In that trial close you told Mr. Castleman that, having learned more about his organization, you thought you could succeed in it. While hoping for some positive feedback, you, wisely, left the door open for any additional issues or questions. Let's say the following potential objection is raised by Mr. Castleman.

"I've enjoyed our meeting, too. You've got a great background, but Southern Beverages is a small organization. What I'm concerned about is that all of your experience is with large companies." This is a fair assessment, and it's one that you should have seen coming as you prepared for this interview. (This is another strong reason to prepare separately for each and every interview. That way you have the time to analyze your strengths and weaknesses relative to each position you're interviewing for, and you don't rely on your generic preparation.)

Remember: you're here for a job, not for a debate. (Plus, if you have my kind of luck, Mr. Castleman is the former captain of the college debate team.) You don't necessarily have to change Mr. Castleman's mind. What you have to do is give his observation its due respect and decide if you can overturn it or if the best you can do is address it. Unless there's some big hole in your resume (that you now must explain), we'll say Mr. Castleman's observation is correct. This means you can't overturn his objection, but you can address it. Here's how.

Take a moment and think through the interviewer's objection and look at it from her perspective. What concerns would you have if you were hiring a big-company person for a job in a small company? With this in mind, a good possible response could be something like this: "I see your point, Mr. Castleman. But in my last job, the leasing group I supervised operated more like an independent business unit. I helped our team develop a real entrepreneurial attitude, and because we had to live off of our own revenues, we all had to wear different hats. I really enjoyed it. In fact, it was that experience that convinced me I could be a lot more successful in an organization like yours."

Okay, maybe you didn't exactly have this kind of experience. What types of entrepreneurial situations *have* you been in? What convinced you that you should work in one now? You must have some good reason for wanting to go from a big company to a small company. (When you prepare for these potential objections remember Figure 4.2, Dr. Paul's Guide to Honesty and Survival. Don't go saying something brutally honest such as "If I had to fill out another requisition form in triplicate for a box of stupid paper clips, I would have gone postal.") Show due respect, think the objection through objectively, respond to overturn or address it, and always wrap up by hitting one of your strong points.

Let's look at another example so I can throw in another wrinkle. Your trial close for the Scruton Animal Clinic job suggested that one element of your background (having dog training experience) would be a strong selling point. Let's say that your trial close has reminded Dr. Scruton of an item from his wish list that suddenly has arisen out of nowhere as an objection to your candidacy. He says, "Yes, dog training experience would be helpful, but we deal with all kinds of animals here, and I was really hoping to hire someone who was working her way through veterinary school." Even though this element may never have come up before, don't panic. Think it through. What is behind this objection? It's not as easy to figure out as the distinction between a large company and a small company. Frankly, it's not clear what the heck he's driving at.

When this is the case, you need to ask a clarifying question. Maybe something such as "I wasn't aware you were looking for a vet student.

I didn't catch that in your ad. What do you hope someone like that would bring to the technician position?" She may say they would be smart or they would have an opportunity to see in practice what was being taught in school or that *she* worked as a vet tech while she was in school or that she *wished* she had been a vet tech or who knows what else. The important thing is that you now have found out what's behind the objection. The rest of the plan stays the same. Offer due respect ("I can see how that would be helpful"). Think it through and respond to overcome or address ("I'm hoping to take some vet tech courses myself after I get a handle on my new work schedule"). Wrap up on a strong point ("But what I hope you consider is that what I'm looking for is a vet tech job—not a stepping stone to something else. Plus, I don't have exams and hospital rotations to worry about, so overtime and the occasional weekend won't be a problem").

When you uncover an objection, the interviewer is not objecting to you as a person. He is giving voice to his fears, his concerns about your potential job performance, or maybe even his biases or stereotypes. These things do exist and it is your job to get them out in the open so they can be dealt with. Otherwise, they will work against you after the interview when you have no opportunity to respond. If you can overcome the interviewer's fears, overturn his biases, and address his concerns, you will discover for yourself that uncovering and handling objections provides you with strong selling opportunities that the other candidates for your job may never get.

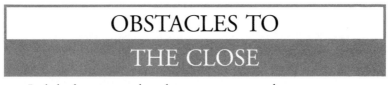

OBSTACLES TO THE CLOSE

Let's look at some obstacles to your strong close.

The Unprepared

You will find some interviewers who are woefully unprepared for you. At first you may think this is good news, but it's really not. You *want* the interviewer to have a handle on what she is actually looking for so you can target your responses accordingly. There are some dim-witted interviewers out there (who obviously don't have enough to do) that keep interviewing a string of folks until it occurs to them that this or that person can probably do the job in question.

Using a trial close to uncover potential objections with these folks is next to impossible. Because they don't have a clear picture of what they are looking for, it is impossible for them to see where you meet their needs and where you don't. And sadly, this is not the only type of resistance you will encounter.

The Control Freak

Some untrained interviewers are afraid the interview will get away from them. They will not let you get a question or a trial close in to save your life. You can recognize this person because he will have an interview outline, usually with 25 or so questions. The plan is that your answers, at approximately two minutes apiece, will take about 50 minutes, and he will try to leave about 10 minutes at the end to answer "any questions you may have."

This is not as bad as it seems. At least he knows what he wants to learn about you. Sometimes, after a comfortable rapport is established (that is, he feels comfortable and in control), you can work in a question. Make your first one something specific you want to learn about the potential assignment or the organization. Then let him ask a few more questions, putting her firmly back in the driver's seat. Only then do you try a trial close.

The Screening Interviewer

Your first interview may be conducted over the phone or in person with a human resources person, or an employment agency, or with someone else not from the department you're hoping to join. These people have been assigned to screen applicants to determine a preliminary list of potential candidates. Typically, they are not the hiring manager for whom you hope to work.

They don't have the appropriate position or the power to hire you. But they will determine whether you continue in the hiring process. So even with screening interviews, it is wise to use a trial close to ensure that there are no objections to your candidacy at this point.

You

These professional sales techniques will not work if you take criticism, negative feedback, or objections personally. It helps to remember that you are essentially an unknown quantity to these strangers who are interviewing you. If they have a potential objection to your candidacy, then you have done an incomplete job of telling them all the wonderful things you can do for them. Their objections have given you a golden opportunity for which you should be thankful.

These professional sales techniques will not work if you don't practice them. Practice includes preparing for potential objections, preparing clarifying questions, and thinking through how to overcome or address each one of them—for every interview you go to. Reading about them isn't enough; thinking about them isn't enough. You need practice so you won't sound artificial.

These professional sales techniques will not work if you don't believe they will work. You won't hurt my feelings if you feel this way, but do yourself a favor and talk to a couple of *successful* professional salespeople (not the new kid at the stereo shop or the new girl at the makeup counter). Ask them if it's true that objections pave the road to sales. Ask them if the best closers are the best sellers. Ask them if they use these skills (they probably do), and if they share their prized closing technique with others (they probably don't). Ask them if they think you (with practice) can learn to use these skills in your winning job interviews—they probably do!

ASK THE BIG
QUESTION

Now that you know what a trial close is, how to uncover potential objections, and how to address or overturn them, it's time for the actual close. In professional sales training it's called *asking the big question*— asking for the sale. Job interviewing isn't exactly like the sales of professional services or products; in traditional sales you would ask for the sale by saying something such as "So Ms. Ethier, we've talked about features, and we've talked about your budget and delivery needs, all of which we can meet. Can we sign an agreement for this system this afternoon?" You have reminded the buyer of what you have discussed and how you have met her objections, and you have asked for the sale.

Now the buyer has to answer yes or give you another objection, which you'll do your best to handle. Then you try again to close the sale. Maybe another objection arises. Again, you do your best to overturn or address it. And back in for the close you go. This might seem almost self-abusive, but some sales trainers suggest that five, six, or seven attempts to close a sale may be needed before a salesperson will get a firm yes or no.

Any seasoned salesperson will tell you that this is the hardest part of the sales process. A lot of salespeople go on and on about what they are selling, but never manage to get to the part where they ask the big question. This is why you will often hear sales managers say that there are many salespeople out there, but damn few good closers out there. You, my winning job interviewee, will be both.

Because very few hiring decisions are made on the spot at the end of the interview, it wouldn't work very well for you to say something along the lines of "Aren't I great? Can I start tomorrow?" You need to be more subtle. But even being appropriately subtle will still bring the job offer closer to you than it will to the job candidate who lets the interview end with a whimper ("Thank you. I hope to hear from you, Mr. Gilroy.") rather than with a good strong close.

Tell 'em You Want It

One of the strongest possible ways to close an interview is to tell the interviewer that you want the job. Hey, that's the reason you're in there for the interview, right? Some folks have debated me on this point. They say they are there to see if there is a good fit, to see if the pay is fair, to see if there is growth opportunity. There is a name for these people: losing job candidates. While they are embarked on this intellectual voyage of discovery, some other job candidate is going to get in there, make a strong presentation, uncover and deal with potential objections, focus on closing the deal, and get the job offer. Then that person will be the one assessing the fit, the compensation, and the growth opportunity. In other words, you can't decide whether or not you'll join the organization until you get the job offer, and that—the offer—is the objective of the interview.

Let's look at a couple of examples of how you might do this. Going back to the Scruton Animal Clinic case, you could use something like the following: "Dr. Scruton, this is exactly the type of job I'm looking for. I have a background working with animals and I'm good with them. I have a strong interest in learning more about the field, and I have the work habits that make me a good team player and a good employee. When you make your decision, I hope you decide to hire me." Whew! How could she resist? She might say she has some more people to interview (often true), that she will not be making her decision until next week, or something else. At that point, stay upbeat, thank her for her time, and reiterate that you look forward to hearing something positive.

For another approach that directly takes into account a possible objection, let's go back to the Southern Beverages example. (Remember that Mr. Castleman had a concern about your lack of small-company experience.) A good close might go something like this: "Thanks for having me in today, Mr. Castleman. I really enjoyed it. Southern Beverages is just the type of organization I'm looking for because here I can combine my solid corporate experience with my natural entrepreneurial drive. If you make the decision to hire me, and I hope you do, you won't be disappointed." If the potential objection seems central to the job, there is no sense trying to dodge it. Try to put a positive spin on it, as in this example, by positioning it as bringing solid business skills to a small, fast-moving company. And then finish up by hitting the strong point of your small-company, entrepreneurial attitude.

The Power of Desire

Do you remember junior high or middle school when a friend told you someone had a crush on you? Regardless of whether or not you had any interest in that person, you now viewed him differently. You might not have been attracted to him, but you couldn't deny his good judgment and taste, right? In some cases, this reappraisal could lead to including this person in your social circle, to a friendship, or even to a relationship of sorts. This is evidence of the impact of being desired, and there are few things as powerful.

Let's move forward to a time in your adult life when you are dating. You have been with someone a while, and she says, "I love you." Regardless of whether or not you are looking or hoping for a long-term relationship, what phrase is it that you instinctively know is the right response? It's not "And I value your friendship," it's not "Super, because I'm having the time of my life," and it's sure as heck is not "Hey, who doesn't?"

The only fully correct response to "I love you" is "And I love you too." And it frequently slips out even when it is not fully true (though sometimes it may be true enough for the moment, if you catch my drift). Again, this is the power of being desired, and asking for the job, pointedly telling the interviewer that you want the job, is one of the strongest closes you can use.

I'm not saying that a strong close will overcome a weak resume or lack of interviewing preparation and practice. I'm not saying it will get you a job for which you're not qualified. But I *am* saying that the fact that you clearly and directly expressed your desire to be hired is guaranteed to stick in the interviewer's mind when he makes the final hiring decision. It's another factor in your favor, and using every one at your disposal is what winning job interviews is all about.

The following diagram will give you a good overview of the two paths to closing an interview.

Figure 6.1

Closing the Interview

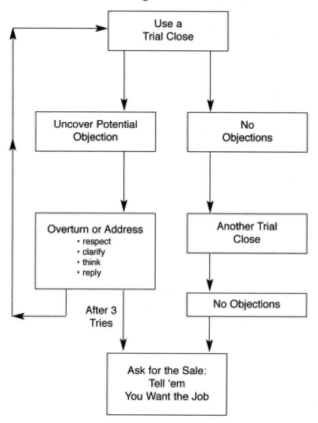

Some Basics to Remember

As the interview winds down and you are focusing on asking good questions, using trial closes, uncovering and overturning objections, and asking for the job, it is sometimes too easy to overlook the basics. These are eye contact, a smile, and a strong handshake.

Because you will have thought over possible objections to your candidacy before the interview, you will have had time to come up with some strategies to deal with them. Thus, when you are in the closing phase of the interview, you shouldn't look as though you are painfully struggling to dredge up the date that the Magna Carta was signed or the ratio of whiskey to sweet vermouth in a Manhattan (1215 and 3:1, respectively). No lip-biting or squinting into space. Relax, breathe smoothly, and make good eye contact to communicate your earnestness and desire.

Your smile should come naturally because, after all, the interview is over. (Just don't sigh deeply and say "whew" under your breath.) A good, solid, dry, firm handshake will end the interview on a strong note. If your hands have perspired during the interview, subtly deal with this before that final handshake. During your interview prep sessions, try out your handshake on your practice partner a few times until you get it right. You're going for firm, not bone-crushing, and enthusiastic, not game-show winner.

BACK TO
CARNEGIE HALL

Like it or not, using effective sales techniques is essential to job hunting and job interviewing. But even the strongest salespeople I know do not automatically transfer these skills into their job interviews. However, from their experience they know enough to practice. Good questions to ask, subtle trial closes, and strategies to overcome possible objections do not just materialize out of thin air during the interview itself. They are pondered, written down, analyzed, practiced, refined, and practiced again well before the interview.

I don't expect these techniques to come to you naturally. This is why tools #9, #10, and #13 in the Toolkit all have elements touching on effective interview-closing techniques. If you use them, you will reduce your interview anxiety, you will improve your interview performance, you will outprepare your competition, and you may just land the job you love.

CHAPTER 7

TURNING THE OFFER INTO A JOB YOU LOVE

Getting a job offer is not like winning the lottery; you're not supposed to act all surprised or speechless or gushing with emotion. The offer is a predictable result of your well-thought-out, four-front job campaign, meticulous preparation, and a winning job interview. With the work you have put into your plan and the preparation you have put into your interview, the job offer should come as no great surprise. And because it doesn't come as a bolt out of the blue, your reaction will be calm, thoughtful, and professional. Don't break out the bubbly just yet, because you still have some work to do.

The offer will most likely be made verbally at the end of the interview or in a follow-up meeting or telephone call. Your initial reaction should be appropriately pleased and appreciative, but you need to be on your guard not to say anything that can be interpreted as an immediate acceptance. It may feel as if you're supposed to immediately accept (or reject) the offer, but, in fact, you are not yet in a position to do this because you don't know the details of the offer. You haven't sufficiently analyzed the job itself, nor have you evaluated the compensation package. Your potential new employer has taken enough time to interview a series of people, think through the decision to hire you, and put this offer together. Certainly you deserve adequate time to make an informed decision.

Most employers and most recruiters understand that you need time to make a decision about the job offer, but they will subtly exert some pressure on you to make a decision "as soon as you can." From their perspective this is a reasonable approach because they have work that needs to be done, they think you are the person to do it, and if you aren't going to accept the offer, they need to approach their backup candidate in the shortest time period possible. Although I want you to take enough time to make an informed decision, I also want you to make it "as soon as you can" so that no one (an internal or last-minute candidate) slips in there ahead of you. You can narrow down this critical time period substantially if you lay the foundation for your decision-making now—before you're on the hot seat with a clock ticking loudly in your ear.

ABOUT THAT CLOCK

If the job offer has been made in person or by phone, it is entirely appropriate to ask for it in writing. In fact, it's customary for them to have an offer package already prepared or ready to send to you. Until you have the offer letter in your hand, you have no offer. They know this, and now you know this. If you get the offer verbally, you can say something such as "That's great, Barbara. I'm really looking forward to getting something in hand so I can discuss it at home and make a decision. What kind of deadline are we working with?"

If you need more time, this is the time to ask for it. You might also add something such as "As soon as I have the offer, you can rest assured that it will be my top priority." Once the clock is ticking, your goal is to beat the deadline. You don't want your new employer to feel that you're holding out until the last minute just because you can.

If you are handed the offer letter at the end of the interview, you can say something such as "Thank you, Barbara. I can't wait to share the good news at home. What kind of deadline are we working with?"

Again, your goal is to beat the deadline, although you have less time to evaluate the offer, as you already hold it in your hot little hands.

A number of single folks have asked me if it isn't a little weird for them to mention sitting down at home to share or discuss a job offer as a way of buying a little time to make an informed decision. Not at all. For all it's anybody else's business, you could be discussing the job offer with your cat. ("Good news, Barfy. It looks like we're trading up to Tender Vittles.") As of the latest issue of the *World News Weekly*, I'm assuming you were not cloned in a lab or beamed down from the Mothership, so you probably have parents or perhaps a brother or sister or crazy aunt or favorite uncle with whom you could discuss your new offer. Today there are any number of different family configurations, and whatever yours is, you get to discuss your job offer with them.

WHAT ELSE IS ON THE TABLE?

A pat on the back is well deserved at this point because all your hard work has finally paid off. But don't let up yet, because, with a little extra effort on your part, you may be able to quickly generate some additional offers or negotiate with your potential new employer to improve the offer you already have in hand. Back in Chapter 2 we discussed how to get more and better interviews, and Figure 2.1 on page 61 demonstrated how the four-front job campaign is designed to help you front-end load the system so you weren't pursuing only one opportunity at a time. This is where that approach really pays off.

Generating Multiple Offers

At this point, you may have other irons in the fire. If you've played your cards right, you have already been in for a first or second interview at a couple of other places, or, a least, have some other good, prospective interviews coming up soon. The bona fide offer you now have gives you the opening to contact these potential employers to see if you can accelerate their hiring process. It may work, it may not work, but it's worth a shot.

To put yourself in the right frame of mind to contact these folks, consider, for a minute, their position. They are working hard to find the right person for an open position and have identified you as a strong potential candidate. Without notifying them of your change in status, you will have reduced their pool of good job candidates, and they don't even know it. If, in fact, you are a leading candidate, their hiring process could be set back weeks, creating more recruiting and interviewing work for them and leaving the work they hoped you would be doing undone. Thus, it is a matter of courtesy to inform other potential employers of your situation and see if there is any way they can bring your candidacy to closure in a reasonable time period.

The best way to do this is with a phone call that could go something such as "Mr. Franklin, thanks for taking my call. At the end of our last interview I know you said you were hoping to get back to me in the next couple of weeks, but there has been a new development that I wanted to bring you up to date on. Another organization that I've been in touch with has just made me a good job offer. But, as you know, I'm very interested in the position with *your* department. Now I know you have more on your plate than just filling this one job, but I was calling to see if we might be able to get together in the next couple of days."

You have courteously updated this potential new employer, you have enhanced your value in his eyes by announcing your job offer, and you have asked for another meeting to (you hope) generate another offer. Here is another instance where human psychology works in your favor. Most folks have a tendency to grasp at that which is about to slip through their fingers. And at this point, that is you. If you are on the short list of job candidates, you will probably get the meeting, and, possibly, another job offer.

Perhaps you have an interview scheduled, but it's a week or 10 days in the future. Or maybe you have no other strong job possibilities at the moment. Presumably, you have been sending resumes and making inquiries to other employers that haven't yet generated interviews.

Make a short list (four to six organizations) of these places and make a call similar to the previous example. Your goals are to, as a courtesy, inform them of your change in status and see if, within a reduced time frame, you can get in there for an interview.

You might try something such as "Ms. Gentile, I'm Amanda Huginkiz. I recently sent my resume to you about that service position you have open. (Or, "I have an upcoming interview with you about the open position in the service department.") Another organization just made me a job offer, but, with everything I've learned about your company, I was really hoping to see if there might be a place for me there. I'm sure you're quite busy, but is there any way we could meet before I have to give my answer to this other company?" This is somewhat less likely to work than if you had already been in for an interview that went well. But I have seen it produce results with enough frequency to know it is something you should try, at least with some carefully targeted employers.

Don't, Don't, Don't

Never try the tactic of using one offer to leverage another if you don't actually have a job offer in hand. It will, in all probability, backfire. If you are playing it fast and loose with the truth (and you are not a compulsive, well-practiced liar), it will probably come through in your voice. Or maybe there is nothing the interviewer can do about her hiring schedule and you now have blown the chance for a potentially fruitful interview at a later date. Imagine how it would feel to hear something such as "Well, Harry, that's great about the offer. We can't really move our process along any faster and we're always sorry to lose a good potential employee. But we sure wish you the best in your new job." Gulp. What do you do now? The answer is you go away sadder but wiser.

EVALUATING
THE OFFER

You may or may not have had some luck generating other interviews or offers. If so, this is great because you can now balance and weigh one offer against another. But even if you have only one offer on the table, it is crucial for you to do a thorough analysis of it. You need to approach this process in a thoughtful manner as devoid of emotion as you can. This is especially difficult if you have been unemployed for a while, because *any* paying job may seem better than being unemployed. As hard as it may be to see it at the moment, this is not true. Unless financial disaster is right around the corner, accepting the wrong job is worse than no job at all because now you have to perform well at the job you accepted while going back out into the job market to find a more suitable position. Oh, and you will need a reasonable explanation of why you are job hunting so soon after having accepted a new position. This is a hard sell and it is best avoided.

Two central elements of any job offer are intimately interwoven: the job itself, and what they are offering to pay you to do it. It is important that you draw a clear distinction between the two so that you can assess them independently. What you are seeking is a balance between a good job that fits with your short- and long-term career goals and a compensation package that is fair for someone with your background, skills, and expertise. By making a calculated, professional, two-pronged assessment of the job offer, you can avoid jumping at a great job for which you will be underpaid (and resentful) or being swept away by a great pay package for a job that you really don't fit (and, ultimately, being miserable). Taking the time to conduct this assessment will put you in a strong position if you need to try to upgrade the position that has been offered, and will certainly be an asset when you negotiate to enhance your compensation package. Let's take the two parts of this assessment in turn.

ANALYSIS
OF THE JOB

I know, I know—I told you to tell them that you wanted the job when you were closing the interview, and now I'm telling you to analyze the job with the critical eye of a pawnbroker. Hey, that's the difference between selling and buying. When you were selling yourself, you were putting the best possible spin on who you are and what you can do. It was *their job* to really dig in and find out what you are all about. Now that they have made you the offer, they are selling you on the job and the organization. Now it's *your job* to really dig in and make doubly sure that this is the job and the organization in which you can succeed.

The Work Itself

In one of the great studies of all time concerning employee motivation, Frederick Herzberg identified *the work itself* as being among the most powerful of workplace motivators. If the work itself is wrong for you, then no amount of money, status, car allowance, signing bonus, or anything else can make it right. You have been thinking about this job (or a job like it) since you began this job hunt. You had certain criteria in your head as you began your search. Your initial research fortified this picture with hard data about where this job might be found and how much you might get paid to do it. You further explored this set of goals through your interviewing process. Now is the time to compare and contrast your goals and targets with the offer or offers you have been able to generate.

The Job Offer Analysis Tool (#14 in the Toolkit) can help you systematically think through the distinct elements of the job you have been offered. It has a number of items that will help you assess the likelihood of your success in this new position. Broadly speaking, they break out into four categories: (1) degree of fit with your current job target(s), (2) your assessment of the organization, (3) degree of fit with your career goals, and (4) how this position will affect your lifestyle. Let's take them in turn.

Fit With Your Job Target(s)

Is the job you are being offered the one you actually discussed in the interview? Will you be doing the things you most want to do? Is this job a step up or a lateral move? Are you ready for this level of responsibility? Is the scope of responsibility more or less than you hoped it might be? Can you tell? How does it fit with your functional, industry, and geographic targets? Have you assessed your relationship with your potential supervisor, peers, and subordinates? How secure do you think this position is? Does it have the status you want? In this job, will you have adequate opportunity to develop your technical and/or management skills? How confident are you that you will succeed in this job? What don't you know about this job, and how can you find it out?

The Organization

It is possible to be offered a job that is just what you've been looking for, but the organization is so dysfunctional that, despite your best efforts, you still can't succeed. To avoid this, you need to get a good overview of the entire organization. What is the history of this organization? What are the organization's prospects for the future? Has it been or could it be bought out, merged, or acquired? What would this mean for your position? What kind of reputation does the company have in the industry, with vendors, suppliers, and contractors, and in the community? What is the organizational culture? How does it treat its people? Does it typically promote from within or is it almost certain that you will have to look outside the organization to get ahead?

Fit With Your Career Goals

The job you are being offered may or may not be your dream job. So be it. The big question is: Will this job help you on your path to ultimate career success? Is this job a step forward in your career, or is it merely a stopgap assignment? Will this job allow you to develop the skills you need to succeed but don't yet have? Does this organization have a supervisory or management development program? How will this job and this employer look on your resume?

Lifestyle Issues

Your new job is going to have an impact on you and your family well beyond the parameters described in the offer letter. One lifestyle issue I hear more and more about is business travel. How much is required, and how much of it is overnight, on weekends, or international? Is this the kind of workplace where you can fly in at 10 or 11 p.m. and be expected at the office at 8:30 a.m.? Do they have a "comp time" (or overtime) policy? What is the vacation policy, and are employees actually encouraged to use it? How often is relocation necessary, and what is the "relo" policy? If you have to relocate, will they help your partner or spouse find a new job? Does the company have a paternity/maternity or family leave policy? Is this organization known as family-friendly or family-unfriendly?

Are We Okay for Launch?

You have looked at this job from every angle you can think of. Perhaps you haven't been able to answer every one of the questions put forth here. Which of those questions are essential for you to have answered before giving this job a thumbs-up or thumbs-down? Where can you find this information? The library, the Web, your network contacts—or will you need another meeting with your prospective employer?

Although this job may not be perfect, it may still be a good career move for you at this specific point in time. My purpose in having you thoroughly dissect this job is for you to know its strengths and liabilities so you can make the best decision possible. I have stressed gathering and assessing hard data, but I also want you to check in with your "gut"—your feelings, your emotions. What are they telling you? Is this job a good one for you now or should you keep looking?

Once you have completed this assessment, you have to make one of three decisions. You may decide that this job is totally wrong for you. If so, you must reject the offer and make a courteous call thanking the interviewer for his time and interest. But don't take this path without thinking it through. You may decide that even though the job isn't perfect, perhaps you can negotiate on enough key issues so that it becomes acceptable. I think this is always worth a try; you have nothing to lose because you have almost decided to reject the offer anyway. Make a list of your bottom-line issues for your negotiation session and move on to evaluating the compensation package. My fervent hope is that you are able to decide that the job that has been offered to you is just what you are looking for. If you are, in fact, sure about the job itself, it is time to look analytically at what they are offering to pay you to do it.

EVALUATING THE COMPENSATION PACKAGE

The most energetic and fortunate job hunters will have generated more than one job offer, which makes the compensation package evaluation process fairly straightforward. With two (or more) bona fide offers on the table, you have concrete data from one that you can directly compare with the other(s). This makes the decision process a bit easier. At the other end of the spectrum is the job hunter who is unemployed and may be having serious financial problems. Her analysis is going to be pretty easy too. (Let's see now: eating versus starving—what to do, what to do?) Fortunately, most folks aren't in this position (or are, at least, a few steps away from it). In fact, even if you are feeling financially strapped, I want you to take some time to fully understand your new compensation package.

What most job hunters face is a situation in which they are generating job offers one at a time regardless of whether they are employed or not. This tends to lead most folks to narrow down the decision criteria to two (that is, current/most recent pay vs. new offer). To help your compensation evaluation process, I recommend that you invest some time and energy *before* you generate your first offer to expand your decision criteria. The Compensation Package Evaluation Tool (#15 in the Toolkit) shows you how to do this.

I want you to compile some specific compensation data well before you generate your first job offer. Start by documenting the elements of your current pay plan. Then, based on the target(s) of this job hunt, determine what you want your new compensation package to look like. Next, I want you to engage in a very enlightening exercise: I want you to evaluate your current cost of living and financial needs (not *wants*) and determine what the minimum compensation package is that you can afford to accept.

This latter set of data is important to have for a couple of reasons. Sometimes a person's dream job is offered, but at a much lower salary than had been targeted. As long as it doesn't lead to financial ruin (that is, cash flow below your cost of living), accepting this offer might be a good decision if it launches you into a great new career or it relocates you to where you've always wanted to live. Financial planners have told me that this is also a useful exercise to help a family determine how much they can really set aside for a secure financial future rather than just burning up pay raises with the purchase of unneeded consumer goods.

Even if you are generating only one job offer at a time, you now have three other compensation packages against which you can compare the one you just received. Some of the compensation elements you see in Tool #15 may not apply to you. There may be some that are unique to your situation that you need to include. But now you have a customized, data-rich tool that can help you make a thoughtful decision about the compensation package you have been offered that minimizes some of the emotional effects that discussions of money can bring.

If the compensation package being offered is not up to what you have set as a target, do not despair. Using your evaluation tool, determine what salary and benefits comprise your bottom line. Add 5 to 10 percent to this and you now have your starting negotiating position. It's good to remember that although most job hunters are hoping for a 20-percent boost in salary, this won't automatically happen just because you are changing jobs. Even if the pay you are being offered is on-target with what you had hoped to get, I recommend that you also add 5 to 10 percent to that number and try to negotiate the offer upward. You may have underestimated the market or the demand for people in your specialty, and it is likely that you were offered a salary somewhere near the middle of the pay range for your position. Either way, you may be able to generate some wiggle room that will put more money in your pocket.

SO YOU WANT...?

Before you contact the person who made you the offer to start negotiating, I want you to have a crystal-clear picture of your negotiating position. Do not go into this thinking you can wing it. They have a lot more practice at this than you do. You have done a comprehensive analysis of the job that has been offered. What is it that you need to accept the job? What is it you are going to ask for? What are you willing to live without? You have evaluated all the elements of the compensation package. You know there is probably some more money on the table if you are willing to ask for it. What is the number you are looking for? What else are you going to ask for? What is the minimum you are willing to accept to do this job?

Take the time to write down the short list of items you want to negotiate. Tell yourself that you are worth what you are asking for. Having a positive, upbeat attitude will help you as you negotiate. You are not going in to beat anyone out of anything. You are looking only for what the market will bear and to do what is best for your career and your family. Regardless of how successful you are in your negotiations, employers understand and accept this.

NEGOTIATING THE OFFER

Negotiations of any kind are always most effective when done face to face. This enables you to see and read facial expressions, monitor changes in body language, and better interpret changes in vocal tone and inflection. You do all of these things almost unconsciously in your everyday conversations, but these data are critical in negotiating so you can better assess what to push for, when to push for it, and how far to push. As I said before, do not go into a negotiating session looking to beat the other person. This "win-lose" attitude will not help you achieve your end goal and can potentially poison your future working relationship. Think "win-win," and it will positively influence your attitude, demeanor, and approach.

First Things First

When you meet to discuss your job offer, start by thanking the interviewer for the opportunity to discus the offer with him. Although most folks want to jump right to the money issue, address the most important job issues first, because you want to be seen as being more interested in succeeding at the job than you are in the money. Once you have the essentials of duties and responsibilities, reporting relationships, staff, resources, and such taken care of, you can then address the compensation package.

You have already identified what it is you are looking for, but it requires a little finesse to get to the point. I suggest you recap all the job issues you have already agreed upon and then segue into the money issue. You might say something such as "That's great, Wayne. Working directly for you to open up three new call centers in the next 18 months, two of which I'll end up running myself, is just the kind of assignment I've been looking for." At this point, ole Wayne is nodding his head positively, agreeing with your description of the job, and expressing satisfaction at having found someone who is a great fit for it. Then you add something such as "I'm really looking forward to the opportunity and I'm confident that I'm the right person for this job, but, as I looked over the offer, I was hoping that there might be some flexibility in the compensation."

Now, ole Wayne doesn't think you mean flexibility for them to pay you less; he knows you mean flexibility for them to pay you more. What's great about an approach such as this is that you can use it whether or not you genuinely need more money before you can accept the job. Even if the pay is fine with you, most employers always leave a little financial wiggle room, expect you to try to find it, and will respect you for your effort. For you to disappoint them would almost be, well, uncivilized. So go for it. This employer now has a vested interest in closing this deal with you, and usually, a little more money can be forthcoming.

Wayne might say something such as "Well, Alyona, what salary did you have in mind?" or, "Okay, Alyona, what's your bottom line?" At this point, it's time to fish or cut bait. Say the number you have in mind. This number should be realistic and based on your earlier research about the field, the function, and this company. Wayne will say one of three things. He will either say something such as "Fine, we can do that," or, "I'm not sure we can do that. I'll need to find out," or he'll say, "Wow, we have a problem because we can't get anywhere near that."

It's great news if he gives the first response, although your immediate reaction will be "D'oh. I should have asked for more." Sorry, Homer, that bus just left and the deal is done. The second response is sort of like a maybe. Treat it as a temporary detour. Say something such as "Great. I appreciate your looking into that for me because we're not really that far apart." Then drop the topic for this discussion, but, before you leave, end with "Can I expect a call on the salary issue?" to show you haven't forgotten about it. If you get the message that you are miles apart, it still may not be a deal-breaker, but you have some fancy footwork ahead of you.

Putting the Deal Together

You may need to bluntly ask the question: "So how far apart are we?" Whatever the number is, don't give up the ship. Try to discover if there is an incentive program or a bonus plan based on performance that could bridge the gap. Explore the extent and value of each item in the benefit plan. You may be pleasantly surprised to learn that a 401(k) plan, company car or car allowance, or other benefits (that is, family dental coverage, or tennis, golf, or health club membership) more than make up the difference, given how benefits are treated by the tax laws. The key is to always stay positive that the deal can be worked out, and always keep throwing ideas on the table. If you are at the high end of the salary range for the job in question, ask if the job can be upgraded so you can be at the lower end of the next range. Ask if a sign-on bonus is possible. Ask if a three- or six-month performance and salary review might be possible. If you don't get defensive and are able to treat this as just another business problem for two motivated people to solve, your attractiveness will only increase.

You may get asked something such as "What is the minimum you would accept?" Do your best to stay away from absolute numbers. I'd try something such as "My compensation (remember, that's salary plus the value of your benefits package) is now in the high 40s, and I'd need something in the low 50s to make this move." Using generic terms such as "low 50s, mid-60s, or high 70s" can help you move a financial step ahead without having your interviewer feel that you are delivering an ultimatum. Ultimatums are always a bad negotiating strategy because very few people like to be leveraged by overt pressure. You want the interviewer to feel that she is directing this process with the ultimate goal of securing your services for the organization. Your role in this process is to help open up every possible avenue to achieve this end.

Unless you are a professional diplomat or labor arbitrator, this negotiating process will feel foreign to you. Before you go in to negotiate your offer, prepare some phrases you think will help you. Try them out on your interview practice partner until you find a few that feel comfortable. Role-play asking for what you deserve. It's a good skill to develop—and not just for the winning job interview!

ACCEPTING
OR REJECTING

Figure 7.1 on the next page gives a systematic overview of how you can best handle the job offers you have so diligently generated. Think about how much time, energy, hard work, and emotional investment it takes to generate one good offer. This is why each and every job offer must be handled with care and professionalism, and be given the respect due a rare and valuable resource. Given the significance of this element of your job hunt, let's quickly review the steps in the winning-job-interview job-offer process.

Figure 7.1

Handling Offers

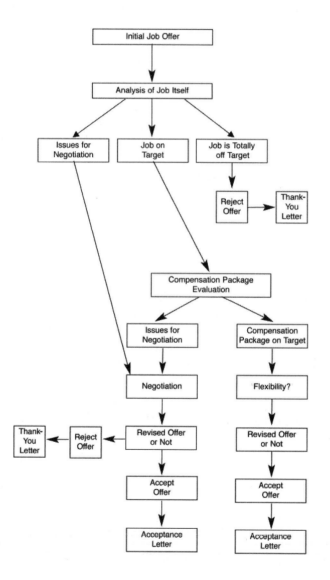

1. Ask for the decision time frame and bargain for more.
2. Prospect for other offers or interviews.
3. Analyze the job.
4. Evaluate the compensation.
5. Set negotiating targets (for the job and for the compensation).
6. Negotiate (in person is best).
7. Decide (accept or reject the offer).

You should communicate your acceptance or rejection of the job offer as soon as you have a firm decision. Your potential employer needs to know if this recruiting and employment task is completed so he can plan for your integration into the rest of the work team or if he needs to start pursuing other candidates for this position. Do your best to beat the decision deadline rather than waiting until the last minute.

Accepting the offer is easy. You do it after deciding that the initial offer is acceptable or after successfully negotiating an improved offer. In person is best, of course, but a phone call will suffice. Try for the personal touch so you can show your enthusiasm. Don't leave your acceptance as a message on voice mail or e-mail. Follow up your verbal acceptance with a formal letter that outlines the terms and conditions of your employment and clarifies your start date.

Rejecting a job offer is a little trickier. There are two points at which you make your rejection decision: either at the point of deciding that the job itself is totally wrong for you, or after unsuccessfully negotiating either the job itself or the compensation package. Although no one likes to deliver bad news on a one-on-one basis, I encourage you to suck it up and talk to the interviewer directly. Convey that this is a business, not a personal, decision; say you're sorry things didn't work out; and thank the interviewer for her time and interest. Do not get drawn into an extended conversation about your decision unless the interviewer is offering to improve the job offer. In the unlikely event that this happens, as with all job offers, ask when you can get it in writing. Do not become negative about the job or the company. The company made you the best offer it could, and it was you who decided not to take it. Do not give the interviewer any negative feedback at all; your rejection is all the bad news she needs for today. Try to leave the conversation on a warm, personal, and appreciative note, because, trust me, you will bump into her or someone she knows later on in your career, and you want her final perception of you to be professional, not snide or snippy. Follow up with a nonspecific but appreciative letter thanking her for her time, and express the hope that you may get to work together at a later point in time.

START SPREADIN' THE NEWS

Another of my counterintuitive rules for winning job interviews is that now, the time between when you accept your new job and the time you actually start it, is a great time to lay the foundation for your next job search. No, I don't mean you should go out and start looking for a new job tomorrow; I mean that how you close out your current job hunt will strongly influence how long it will take and how much energy it will take to get you up and running on your next job search, regardless of when it comes to pass.

Compile or clean up your list of all the contacts you made during your job hunt. This includes everyone in your contact network and the people to whom they introduced you, your reference librarian helpers, every recruiter you contacted (regardless of whether they helped you or not; maybe next time they will), the facilitators of every job search support group you attended, your job references, the Webmaster for every career Website you used, every professional or technical association whose job listings you used, the company recruiting managers you contacted, and everyone with whom you interviewed. In short, this is your new, improved, and expanded career network. Never again will it be as short, as small, or as thin as it was when you started this job hunt.

Prepare a letter that will go to this list of people that thanks them for all their help during your recent job search. Obviously, you will need to personalize this letter for your most helpful and supportive contacts. Let everyone know what job you landed and how they can contact you. Send this mailing about a week after you have started your new job—no sense jinxing things at this point, eh?

Shortly after you start your new job, make a contact in the marketing or public relations department and see if it is appropriate to compile a press release to send to the business press, professional associations, or even just your hometown newspaper. You have just achieved success in a demanding and competitive process, and you deserve all the recognition you can get. This, of course, raises your professional profile and will contribute to the continued success of your career. The Job Search Wrap-up Tool (#16 in the Toolkit) will help you professionally conclude this job search at the same time you are laying a solid foundation for your next one.

CHAPTER 8

GLITCHES, POTHOLES, CALAMITIES, AND IDIOTS

Throughout this book I have shared my optimism in your ultimate career success, my enthusiasm for your job hunt, and my confidence in your ability to develop into a winning job interviewer. I have counseled you into investing considerable energy in your job hunt. I have coached you to lower your interview anxiety by outpreparing your competition. I have demanded that you take ultimate responsibility for your job-hunting and job-interviewing success. At every turn I have urged you to take the high road. I have tried my best to motivate you to, as the old song goes, "accentuate the positive" because a can-do attitude can make all the difference between a job and a career that you love, and the majority of employees who live sad lives of quiet desperation.

When I meet with job hunters to debrief them over a couple of adult beverages after a successful job search, the greatest laughter usually emerges from the things that didn't go so well—the errors, the mistakes, the glitches. They occur in every job hunt, and yours will be no different. The key here is to take everything in stride, prepare for as many eventualities as you can, and, when faced with an interview predicament, stay positive and give it your best shot. You don't have to be perfect, you only have to be better than the other candidates for this one particular job.

With luck, you may never run into an unusual interview format, be asked trick questions, stumble badly in an interview, or meet up with the dreaded idiot interviewer. But this book isn't about luck; it's about you being able to turn any interview into a *winning* job interview regardless of any pothole or calamity you may encounter.

UNUSUAL INTERVIEW FORMATS

Thus far, the only interview format we've talked about is the face-to-face, one-on-one interview. There are a few others for which you need to be prepared.

One Ringy Dingy

Another common interview format is the telephone interview. It is often used as a tool to screen applicants before a face-to-face meeting is scheduled. This is standard practice for both contingency recruiters and retained search consultants. Because you use your phone every day for mundane purposes, it is easy to take this interview casually. Huge mistake! You're not ordering Chinese food here, bucko; you're trying to get your foot in the door with an important job target. This phone meeting is as important as a face-to-face meeting because if you don't do well in the first one, you won't even get to try the other.

The two keys to mastering the phone interview are preparation and physical setting. Before your phone interview, review your research notes, your resume, and the short list of questions you want to ask. Have a clean pad of paper ready and put the interviewer's name and title on it. That way you won't use the wrong name (it's easy to do when you're not actually looking at someone), and you'll have a convenient place to take notes. If an unexpected call for a phone interview comes in, try to reschedule it. Say you were *just* on your way out for a meeting. You wouldn't go into a face-to-face interview on the spur of the moment, so why would you wing it now? Even if you bump the call out for just 10 or 20 minutes, you will be that much better prepared.

Speakerphones are great as long as they don't sound as if you are underwater or on a police bullhorn. If you have a speakerphone, try it out on someone who will give you brutally honest feedback before you ever use it in an interview. If yours sounds clear and crisp, use it, because it will allow you to take notes and use your hands to gesture with as you speak. You may not have noticed it before, but hand gestures and facial expressions add variety to your voice and make you sound more engaged and easier to listen to. I know this may sound corny, but take a lesson from successful telemarketers and keep a mirror on your desk to remind you to smile. A person on one end of the phone can tell when the person on the other end is smiling, because smiling uses muscles that change the tone of one's voice—for the better.

Using a speakerphone presupposes that you have a private, quiet place from which to take phone calls. I have never had an interviewer tell me that listening to a screaming baby, yapping dog, or whining vacuum cleaner made a job candidate sound more professional. It may induce pity, but not a job offer. If humanly possible, avoid conducting a phone interview (or, God forbid, a negotiating session) on a cell phone. Imagine your panic after answering a question brilliantly only to hear your interviewer saying, "Are you there? Can you hear me? Are you there? Hello?" Again, most of these are little points to help you sound more attractive to a potential employer, but all these little points add up in your favor.

Beam Me Up, Scotty

If you are not reading this book from front to back (which is your perfect right) you may be unaware that video conferencing/video interviewing is discussed at some length in the New Tools/New Approaches section of Chapter 2. There you will find the reasons for its growing popularity and how best to utilize this technology before, during, and after the interview.

The Group Grope

They're really called *panel interviews*, and I truly dislike them. (I have to learn not to repress my true feelings.) You meet with a group of three or more interviewers, and each of them takes a turn asking you a question. Not completely unlike the Spanish Inquisition. Sometimes *all* of them are interested in *every* answer, sometimes *some* of them are interested in *all* of the answers, sometimes *some* of them are interested in *some* of the answers, and sometimes they are only interested in the answer to the question they asked. And sometimes there's a poor sap in there who doesn't know why he's there or what he's interested in because he only showed up because his boss told him to "sit in." Just freakin' great! You don't know who wants to hear what. You'll end up directing your answer to the person who asked the question while looking around and trying to make some eye contact with the others who seem interested without having your head swivel around like that girl in *The Exorcist*.

Although you know who arranged the interview and who is likely to be your boss, it is impossible to know the relationships (personal or reporting) among all of them. Sometimes there will be people in a group grope that have competing agendas or different ideas of what they are looking for, or even disagreements on the dimensions of the job itself. Hiring organizations waste time and energy in these kinds of situations, but, even so, you can turn this to your advantage.

If you learn beforehand that you are in for a panel interview, do your best to find out who is participating, why they are participating, and what, if any, specific interest they have in how this job is filled. If something like this is sprung on you when you arrive for the interview (which already gives you some not-so-great feedback about the organization), make it your first agenda to go around the room asking for (and writing down) people's names and titles. Be pleasant about it (because you can't do anything about it anyway), expressing pleasure in meeting them, and, if you can manage it, also ask each of them how they or their department will be involved with the person to be hired. If you're able to do this, you can probably tailor your responses appropriately. If you end up answering questions pretty much in the dark about whose agenda is what, just play it straight down the middle and hope for the best.

The Cattle Call

As grim as this interview sounds, it's a heck of a lot better than the group grope. The formal name is *serial interviews*. You complete one interview and then move right on to someone else. Typically, this doesn't happen until a second or later interview, but if you find yourself being walked down the hall to "meet" someone else after your first interview, you can bet it's good news for you. Either somebody else saw your resume, was impressed, and asked to see you when you came in, or that person told your interviewer to bring you around if she was impressed enough to think about hiring you.

Serial interviews can be draining, but they are a great opportunity for using your winning job interview skills. It is important to keep your energy level high because you are actually making a series of first impressions. As in the panel interview, the key is to get a quick read on who these people are, what their agenda is, and why they are interested in this new hire. You can ask similar questions of multiple folks, and, as you think about the answers afterward, you will learn a lot about the organization. Remember to ask each person for his card so you have the correct information to send personalized follow-up letters.

"Ve Hof Vays of Makink You Talk"

I'm a little conflicted about whether my thoughts on stress interviews belong here or in the section on the dreaded idiot interviewer. Let's deal with it now. Because so much is potentially at stake, every interview is stressful to some degree. That's why I spent so much time earlier in this book showing how to reduce your interview anxiety. A typical interview with the typical amount of jitters is not what we're talking about here. By "stress interview" I mean one that is conducted in an impersonal, brusque, or hostile manner that is meant to intimidate you and throw you off of your prepared, winning interview plan.

The rationale (and I use this word loosely) for the stress interview is that the position you are applying for can be quite stressful, so they want to see how you deal with stress. This is the kind of idiocy you hear from people who don't even have a nodding acquaintance with either logic or human behavior. A stress interview doesn't measure how one deals with on-the-job stress, it demonstrates how you deal with stress interviews—that's it. They are two totally different things.

Stress interviews are opportunities for small, insecure people to inflict their latent aggression on others whom they see as having less power. This is a human flaw that's as old as the needlessly brutal prison guard and as current as the college fraternity hazing deaths we see every year. The only two cases I can think of in which a stress interview would be a useful predictor of on-the-job performance would be if you were seeking a job as a PR person who had to tell the media why your employer was dumping cancer-causing chemicals in the drinking water, or you were applying for a legal position in which you had to defend an executive who squandered stockholder's money on stuff such as $6,000 shower curtains or ice statues that tinkle vodka. And you don't really want those jobs, do you?

Because you might run into a stress interview, you need to recognize and start dealing with it right off the bat. Early signs of a stress interview include situations in which the interviewer doesn't make eye contact, doesn't engage in any initial pleasantries, doesn't ask you to be seated, doesn't shake hands, or starts with a rude remark such as "Okay, let's get this done." Stay cool, stay focused, and stay courteous, because this will thwart her goal of throwing you off balance. Ask yourself what really gets under the skin of that driver who just cut you off: flipping him the bird, or a jovial laugh and wave?

The questioning may become increasingly negative or hostile. As I discussed earlier, never let them put negative words in your mouth. If asked a question such as "Well, if your current company is so great, why are you bailing out?" don't be afraid to reframe the question in your answer. Try something such as "You're right. I'm lucky to have been associated with Acme Anvil Corp., but I've learned as much as I can there, and now I'm hoping that Coyote Rocket Sleds, Inc., can offer me some new challenges." If one of your answers is rudely contradicted, don't be shy about saying something such as "Well, I guess reasonable people can disagree," or, "I guess we can agree to disagree about that one." Always deliver these responses with a friendly smile.

If the rude behavior reaches a point at which you must say something, here's what I advise. Make a friendly but quizzical expression and say, "Excuse me, but is this one of those stress interviews? I saw them mentioned in a book by management psychologist Dr. Paul Powers, but I've never seen one before." This will throw her off balance and perhaps she'll decide to knock off the BS. If she asks you what I said about stress interviews, just laugh and say, "You don't want to know," or, "How 'bout I tell you that after I'm hired."

The Trained-Bear Interview

This is the interview in which you are asked to perform. This could involve role-playing a sales call, answering an angry customer's phone call, or responding to an e-mail or memo that just (hypothetically) arrived. As long as these exercises are within the area of your expertise, they represent a great opportunity to display your skills. Afterward, express your interest in the exercise and ask why that particular example was chosen and how the interviewer thought you might have handled it differently. That way, regardless of how you actually did, you are demonstrating your interest in the problems of the organization as well as showing your willingness to take feedback.

When these trained-bear interviews can be abusive is when employers use the interview process to troll for new ideas that they may use with or without you. Ad agencies sometimes ask an applicant to outline a potential campaign for a specific new client. Consulting firms may ask for a project proposal. I have seen marketers asked to submit two or three concepts for a forthcoming product launch. Graphic designers are often asked to design something "on spec" that the firm will turn around and try to sell. Although assessing your skills as accurately as possible is perfectly acceptable, pilfering your ideas for profit is not. Some companies are well known for this, and your contact network should be able to help you identify them.

If you find yourself in such a situation, you have to decide two things: do you really want to work there, and, if so, are you willing to risk them ripping you off? If the answer to both is yes, then go ahead and submit your ideas, all clearly labeled in small print with "Copyright © [year] by [your name]. All rights reserved." For more details, visit the U.S. Copyright Office online at *www.copyright.gov*. This may give them pause before they rip you off. It also protects your rights if, later, you see your ideas in a magazine or on TV and decide to do something about it. If someone, upon seeing your copyright, has the audacity to ask, "Don't you trust us?" just brush it off with a casual "It's just standard business practice."

Behind the Potted Palm

Job interviews can take place in such different places as hotel lobbies, restaurants, airline lounges, or convention hospitality suites. The biggest problem with these settings is the excess audio and visual stimulation. This makes concentration difficult and can obscure your ability to completely observe or hear your interviewer. Also, because some of these settings are ones in which you might tend to relax, you may let your guard down and treat the meeting with less formality than it deserves. In any of these settings, do your best to establish appropriate eye contact, and do not hesitate to ask your interviewer to repeat a question if you are not sure you heard it completely. There's nothing as confusing or frustrating as giving a great response to the wrong question.

An interview outside of the interviewer's office is usually a good sign that he is trying to fit you into a busy schedule. On the other hand, a lot of executive recruiters are road warriors of the first degree, and hotel lobbies or airline lounges are de rigueur interview locations. Meals can be tricky, but are easily handled with a few simple rules. No finger food (ribs, corn on the cob, raw shellfish), nothing messy (salads, cereal, runny eggs), no booze (sorry), no sending food back, and no ogling or verbal abuse of the waitstaff. Order something similar to that of your interviewer unless it's from one of the categories mentioned here. Don't gesture with your cutlery as if you were a knife thrower from the circus. Oh, and keep in mind all that other stuff your mother told you: keep your elbows off the table, don't talk with food in your mouth, and no making a party hat with your napkin.

Seriously, though, if you feel uncertain about the social graces, there are plenty of etiquette books in the library, but don't obsess about it. All the formality you'll need is to work your way from outside to inside with the cutlery and make an X with your knife and fork on your plate if you're still eating or parallel park them at the 4 or 5 o'clock position if you're done.

After presentations, I often get a handful of questions about the do's and don'ts of how to handle alcohol at a dinner interview. To play it safe, I suggest you completely avoid it. It dulls the mind, it slows your responses, and makes you think you can sing. Despite the relaxing setting, you are not there to have fun; you are there to land a job. If pressed, you can say that you'll be driving later. If it's clear that you won't be driving later, you can say that you have some work to do or some e-mails you need to deal with later. If asked (as I once read in a snotty headhunter's book) if you have a problem with alcohol, avoid the temptation to give a snide reply and instead say, "No; I just prefer not to when working." This response works great and is quite useful if you are a teetotaler or are in recovery. Since the last edition of this book, I have been advised that if you are being interviewed at dinner for a position in the hospitality or adult beverage industry, it is wise to take your lead from the interviewer. This can be tricky, and I suggest you discuss the issue beforehand with someone senior to you in the industry whose judgement you trust.

TRICK
QUESTIONS

There are a few types of trick questions you should know how to handle. Some are asked quite innocently, and others are asked with a definite agenda in mind. One not-so-innocent question concerns proprietary information you may have learned in your most recent job. If asked something along these lines, you can always say something such as "Though I have a solid working knowledge of all areas I was involved with, I certainly wouldn't want to put you, this company, or me in hot water over a proprietary issue." This displays your sense of business ethics and alerts the interviewer that pursuing this line of questioning puts everyone at risk.

Yin or Yang

Another trick question is the forced choice question: one that is asked in such a way that you can choose between only two answers. A couple of examples are: "Are you more of a small-company or large-company person?" and "Are you more comfortable as a leader or as a follower?" The best way to handle this type of question is to be aware of the requirements of the job for which you are interviewing and tilt your answer in that direction. It never hurts to expand your answer a little and mention that you also see value in the option you didn't choose. You might say something such as "Actually, I see myself as more of a leader because I like to take responsibility for making things happen. But the reality is that every boss has a boss all the way up to the president, who answers to the shareholders, so I know it pays to be a good team player as well as a team leader." Or the reverse: "Frankly, at this stage of my career the reality is that I'm more of an individual contributor, and I realize that. But I've learned a lot from working for a couple of strong leaders and that's where I'm hoping my career will go."

What If?

Hypothetical questions are easy to ask and hard to answer. These are the "What would you do if...?" questions. You hear reporters ask political candidates a lot of them. They make the interviewer seem insightful and give candidates plenty of rope with which to hang themselves. They're entertaining to watch on TV, but not especially good news for the job hunter. The only easy hypothetical questions are ones about ethics. (It goes without saying that you always take the high road on questions about ethics.) The big problem with hypotheticals is that there are usually not enough facts or background given to help you put a really cogent answer together. Thus, you're sort of taking a shot in the dark.

The winning job interviewee can put this to work in her favor by spinning out a couple of brief, but (and this is important) *different* answers to a hypothetical question, and then add "Of course, these are only a couple of possible responses. Given all the variables in this situation that I don't know about, there are probably some other, perhaps better, options. I guess that's where I'd really start—getting all the data first, before deciding on a course of action." Another reason to hedge your response to a hypothetical question is that it might concern an internal issue that your prospective employer is facing at that very moment. If you come down on the wrong side of it, you could be doing yourself some damage.

From Way Out in Left Field

We've all heard stories about interviewers who ask inane questions. Although the category is endless, the following are a few actual interview questions job hunters have shared with me.

* ✳ "If you could be a tree (or animal), what type would you be?"
* ✳ "Do you believe in UFOs?"
* ✳ "What weighs more—a ton of iron or a ton of feathers?"
* ✳ "Do you read your horoscope?"

No matter how stupid a question seems, I heartily suggest that you stifle your urge to break out laughing at your interviewer. (Save that for happy hour with your pals.) Your interviewer may have asked the question as an icebreaker. He may have asked the question because somebody asked it of him years ago and he thought it was cool. He may have asked it out of nervousness. He may have asked it because he couldn't think of anything else to ask. Or he may have asked it to see how you deal with inane situations. Who knows?

My suggestion is to tread carefully, say nothing provocative, and play it safe with a generic answer. Even if you genuinely believe in little green men or have always secretly wanted to be a badger, I'd keep these thoughts to yourself. If you get hired, they'll find out soon enough just how weird you really are. No sense rushing things.

The Dreaded Idiot Interviewer

Asking an occasional inane question does not automatically qualify someone as the dreaded idiot interviewer. Repeatedly asking stupid questions will, however, do the trick. Asking overly personal questions or asking questions of an overtly political or religious nature certainly qualify. And asking clearly illegal questions is the hallmark of the dreaded idiot interviewer.

Dr. Paul's Law of the Distribution of Jerks and Idiots says "Jerks and idiots are distributed more or less evenly throughout society." This is good news; otherwise, we would probably have entire towns or companies composed only of jerks and idiots. Having a few jerks here and a couple of idiots over there dilutes the negative effect these clueless folks have on the rest of us. It gives us hope that society won't end up looking like the guests on *Jerry Springer*. But it also means that every now and then you will run into a jerk or an idiot, and this includes your job interviewers.

It's hard to be a winning job interviewee when the person asking the questions is a loser, but it can be done. Early on in this book you learned that if you take the advice and counsel I have offered, you will probably be much more skilled in interviewing than the person who is interviewing you. Sometimes well-intentioned but unskilled people make mistakes. Keeping this in mind will prevent you from jumping down the throat of the interviewer at the sound of the first idiotic or potentially illegal question.

If you hear a question that strikes you as inappropriate, there are a couple of approaches you can try. I suggest that you first consider how a bluntly honest answer might affect your candidacy, and, if you see no problem, answer it. Otherwise, try to redirect the question into fair territory. If you are asked if you are married or dating or plan to have children, you might respond with "I keep my work life and personal life separate. I have no problem with the time investment required by this job or the travel that we discussed, if that's what you're asking." The interviewer may have had that perfectly acceptable concern but didn't know how to ask the question in a legal manner. An illegally phrased question about religion might be masking legitimate issues of your availability to work certain hours or days. A question about national origin or citizenship might be a bobbled attempt at compliance with changing immigration laws or security clearance regulations. By giving the interviewer the benefit of the doubt, you may be able to prevent his interviewing incompetence from preventing you from getting a job that you really want. Keeping a cool head and responding in a civil, forthright manner while helping an interviewer out of a hole he inadvertently dug for himself can win you many points.

If you continue to get questions that make you uncomfortable (two is my limit, but you might have a bit more tolerance than I do), it is time for another, more assertive approach. You might respond with "Mr. Burns, I'm very interested in this position because I think it's a great fit between what you need and what I have to offer. I want to remove any doubt about this that you have, but, frankly, I don't see the relevance of that question to this position." This is a clearly confrontational response, but I suggest you keep the tone professional and assertive and don't cross the line into personal and aggressive. Your goal in this (and in every) interview is to generate a job offer, even if you ultimately reject it or use it only to help you generate other offers. I am not suggesting that you submit to a single iota of abuse or illegal discrimination; at all times you retain the ultimate power of terminating the interview and leaving.

If you do walk out or afterward feel that your rights were violated, what do you do? Complain to the authorities, write a letter to the editor, inform your network, file a lawsuit? This is a very personal decision and I can't make it for you. As your career coach—someone who is 100-percent focused on your career success—I'd have to say walk away and find a better job in a better organization with a better boss. Don't get mad; don't get even. Get ahead. Living well is the best revenge.

But that advice is coming from a guy who never saw a N.I.N.A. (No Irish Need Apply) sign in a shop window, who was never shunted to a separate water fountain or restroom, who hasn't sat at the curb in a wheelchair trying to figure out how to get to a third-floor interview, and who has never worried that his accent labels him as a potential terrorist. After leaving an interview in which you think (not just feel) that you were asked illegal questions, you must first determine if those potentially unlawful questions were asked for the purpose of discriminating against you because of an illegal reason or had the net effect of discriminating against you.

As an interviewer becomes more interested in hiring you, it is natural for her to want to know more about you as a person. (Refer back to Figure 3.2 in Chapter 3.) This helps the interviewer to "make a clear distinction" (the first definition of the word *discriminate*) between you and other candidates. If an interviewer asks a stupid or illegal question—say, about your having children—but the employer has an exemplary record for hiring and accommodating working parents, then any legal action you take will most likely be fruitless, time consuming, and stressful, and won't do your career any good. The nub of the legal issue is that though it is clearly stupid to ask illegal questions, it is not necessarily illegal to ask stupid questions.

If you feel that it is your duty to raise questions about potential illegal discrimination, contact your state employment or equal opportunity agency and the federal EEOC (Equal Employment Opportunity Commission) simultaneously. Typically, the feds defer to the state agency to make the preliminary inquiries, and your filing needs to be within 180 days (by which date I hope you are gainfully employed). These agencies are woefully underfunded and have a huge backlog of cases, and I have seen some of these cases go on for years. Even if nothing comes of your complaint, you may be called to offer testimony at a later date, when an even more egregious violation comes to light.

The legal route is a tough road to go, but you may decide that you have no choice but to pursue it. One former job hunter who called in to my radio show talked about facing this choice. He was insulted enough that he couldn't drop the issue, but he was wary about risking his career options, upon which his extended family depended. He created a third path forward by harnessing his psychic energy around this issue by helping to establish a mentoring and tutoring program for kids in his church from single-parent homes. He didn't merely get mad; he didn't try to get even; he helped others to *get ahead*. As another option, maybe something like this would work for you.

POSSIBLE INTERVIEW CALAMITIES

I say *possible* calamities because most problems that arise in an interview can be fixed. (It takes a little work and you have to stay cool, but issues usually can be resolved.) For example, sometimes miscommunication happens. If you mistakenly arrive an hour early for an interview, you can always excuse yourself and go for a walk. (This is much better than sitting and waiting in the lobby because you can dissipate your nervous energy.) If (gulp) you mistakenly arrive an hour late for an interview, apologize profusely (regardless of whose fault it was), say how much you were looking forward to the meeting, and offer to reschedule at their convenience. On the few occasions I've heard of this happening, they have just gone ahead with the interview.

Resume Errors

I've already cautioned you about having any inaccuracies on your resume: at some point they will be discovered. These errors cast doubt on everything else on your resume and raise questions about your truthfulness in general. But we're all human and mistakes happen. A minor error such as a date that is off by a year is not the same as listing an academic degree you never received or an employer for whom you never worked. The former you can pass off as a typo (still an issue on this important document), but the latter is a deal-breaker. You can try to hem and haw, but if you included this data on purpose, you've done it more than once and you won't be able to blame it on some grievous secretarial error. Accept that you've been found out and exit as gracefully as you can, sadder but wiser.

Fuhgedaboudit

No matter how you try to reduce your interview stress, some of it is going to creep in. If it contributes to keeping you alert and on your toes, that's great. But sometimes it can get in the way of remembering some of your best-prepared responses or your most telling anecdotes or your most insightful questions. This is the sort of brain freeze that happens when someone makes a snide remark to you and a killer comeback doesn't come to you until later that evening. During the ride home after every interview, there will be a moment when you make a fist, tap it on your forehead and say, "Ooh, why didn't I say...?" Or, even worse, you say, "What was I thinking when I said...?"

There is an easy way to fix either of these problems: the thank-you/follow-up note. It should look professional (typed, spell-checked, printed on good paper if sending hard copy), use the correct spelling of the person's name and correct title (check this with the business card you asked for), and be sent immediately after the interview. Along with your new or revised comments, you should reiterate your appreciation for the interview and strong interest in the job. Although particularly helpful in the situations described in the previous sections, this is something you should do after every interview. It's just one more way of communicating "I'm thorough, I'm really interested, and I'm courteous." It's like getting one more chance at bat after the inning is over.

Dem Rattlin' Bones

All of us have an episode that we hope won't show up when they make the made-for-TV movie out of our lives. It may be as unimportant as a lampshade on your head at the office party; it may be as personal as an ugly divorce; it may be as serious as a bankruptcy; or it may be as germane as being fired from your last job. It could be something silly or stupid that was once on a social networking site. Ask yourself, "What is it I really hope I will never get asked about in a job interview?" Write that question down and then prepare an emotionally neutral, factually accurate response that doesn't dwell on the event or delve too far into it. If there is a skeleton rattling away anywhere in your closet, some time, somewhere, a skilled, insightful interviewer will dig it up. It's nothing to lose sleep about as long as you have adequately prepared for it.

YOU WANT TO

KNOW WHAT?!

Some organizations do not rely solely on interviews and references to evaluate job candidates. Many use various testing methods. Some are useful, some are not, but you should know what to expect if you run into them.

Drug Tests

It is now quite common to find the question "Do you consent to take a drug test as a condition of employment?" on company application forms. If you check *no* (and it is noticed), you will probably no longer be in the running for the job in question. You and I may debate the ethics, legality, and appropriateness of this fact, but we need to intelligently face this modern reality. If you check *yes*, sometimes this is the last you ever hear of it. However, most of the time you can expect to be asked to supply a urine sample for testing after you have accepted the job offer but before you actually start your new job.

I wish I could say, "Just don't do drugs and you'll have nothing to worry about," but I can't. The problem is the unacceptable rate of "false positive" results that these tests produce. A "false positive" result is one that shows a non-drug-using test subject as a drug user. The estimated rate of false positives range between 5 percent (in tightly controlled research settings) to more than 50 percent! There are a number of reasons for this. Some pastries and bagels contain poppy seeds that will show up as morphine. Many common over-the-counter medications contain ibuprofen, which may have you test positive for marijuana. Some popular nighttime cough and cold medications will have you test positive for opiates. And, naturally, any medications legally prescribed by your physician for a range of conditions can be expected to show up as well. And we haven't even touched on the issues of unregulated testing labs, poorly supervised testing protocols, or minimum-wage lab workers holding your professional reputation in their minimally trained hands. And yet more companies, government agencies, and unions are mandating these tests. So what are you to do?

First of all, for all the reasons we know so well, don't do illegal drugs. If you are faced with a drug test, here is your strategy. State that you don't use illegal drugs and that you don't object to the test *per se*. But add that you have read about the alarmingly high rate of false positives that they generate. Then ask a few questions:

1. Is this testing program run by a physician (sometimes called an MRO, or medical review officer)? A competent, well-trained medical person is apt to handle the test more professionally than somebody fresh from the muffler shop.

2. Does this testing program use only federally certified testing labs?

3. In the event of a false positive, do I have the right to a retest?

4. Are the results sent elsewhere or are they retained with complete confidentiality?

If you are given a form to fill out asking about which medications you have taken ("recently" or "within the last week"), go back three weeks (because some compounds stay in your body that long) and list every prescription, every over-the-counter medicine, and every nutritional supplement you may have used during that time. Oh, and double-check to make sure that your, ahem, "sample" is accurately labeled so it won't get confused with the one from the guy with the dancing-bear tattoo.

We all have a right to a drug-free workplace, and if you doubt this, consider how you'd feel wondering if the pilot of your next airplane trip or the driver of the huge dump truck next to you on the freeway or the doctor delivering your baby or the cop on the street corner is high. Drug-testing programs are here to stay and will continue to improve in quality and reliability. Who knows, one day companies and the government may even choose to address alcohol abuse at work, which is estimated to cost 10 times more than drugs in accidents and lost productivity.

Psychological Tests

Many organizations conduct psychological assessments of the leading candidates for key positions. Done professionally, this is a moderately expensive process, so the good news is that if you are asked to complete a battery of assessment tools, you have definitely made the short list of candidates. On the other hand, there is a fair share of useless so-called assessment tools, and many "consultants" out there selling assessment services with minimal or no psychological training. At best, a well-conducted assessment can closely determine the degree of fit between you and the needs of the hiring organization. At worst, it can be no more effective than someone trying to read the bumps on your head. In any event, it is another hurdle for you to jump before landing the job for which you have been working so hard.

As with drug testing, I suggest you express your willingness to participate, and then follow up with a few informed questions:

1. Is the person conducting the assessment a licensed psychologist or psychiatrist? Other "testers" may or may not have adequate training and access to the best tools, and are not bound by rigid ethical and professional guidelines.

2. Does he have an extensive background in employment and human resources? Many great shrinks out there have little knowledge of the world of work. A licensed psychologist with experience in this area will use only assessment tools that are statistically reliable and valid, and that are appropriate for the situation.

3. Will the person conducting the assessment explain the tools to you, or do you have to take them "blind"? There is no secret voodoo to bona fide assessment tests, and there is no reason why a competent professional wouldn't fully explain her purpose to you.

4. Are these tests being used as a thumbs-up or thumbs-down on your selection? Psychological testing is best used as part of a three-legged assessment process that also includes the results of personal interviews and data gathered from job references.

5. Whether or not you are hired, will the person who conducted the assessment share the results with you? Some will; others will not. If asked, I share the information with an unsuccessful candidate because I feel it can help the person as he continues with his job search. If the person is hired, I try to arrange a meeting with the new boss and the candidate to use the data to facilitate the assimilation process.

I've been asked if you can or should try to "fool" these tests. Generally speaking, I'd say no. Although you can slant your responses somewhat, the best tools have internal measures for inconsistency, guessing, or faking. Further, I'd have to ask you why you would want a job for which you weren't really suited. That said, I do have a success strategy for you to use when asked to take a psychological assessment battery.

Before you take the tests, do this exercise. Close your eyes and think of the best couple of days you have ever had at work. Now open your eyes and make a list (nouns, verbs, adjectives, it doesn't matter) that describes you on those occasions. Do this a couple of times. Close your eyes again. Picture in your mind's eye a day sometime in the future when you are really succeeding at the job for which you are testing. Open your eyes and add to your self-descriptive list.

Now you have a comprehensive list of the qualities and traits to emphasize in the testing. You are not being asked to reveal every little thing about every aspect of your life. You are being assessed for personality and certain work behaviors such as leadership, independence, and decision-making style. You are a person of many colors, but only certain ones come out at work (or come out most frequently at work), and your best colors shine through on your best days. By keeping your best days in mind, your "true colors come shining through."

Integrity Testing

If I haven't stirred up a hornet's nest yet, this next section should do the trick. It's a fact that American industry loses tens of billions of dollars a year from employee theft. (I saw one article that suggested the number might be as high as $50 billion, and it didn't take into account the growing spate of *executive* piracy.) It's natural that employers would want to address this issue on the hiring side of the problem at the same time they address it with stronger monitoring of current employees. This has given rise to the whole (lucrative) area of honesty, or integrity testing, which has about as much usefulness as the old test for witches. The accused witch was bound hand and foot and thrown in the river. If she floated, she *was* a witch. If she didn't float, she *wasn't* a witch. Either way this poor person had a *really* bad day because the likelihood was that if she didn't die by hanging or burning, she would probably die by drowning. The key, it seems, was the same one I devised long ago for high school chemistry: try to get out of taking the test if humanly possible. The same goes for integrity testing.

Hook Me Up, Baby

Let's take the most famous test in this category: the polygraph, also known as the lie detector. This is a machine that detects changes in such physiological reactions as blood pressure, heartbeat, and respiration. The research is mixed on whether these changes, in fact, indicate whether a person is lying. In folks who are basically honest, it shows physical discomfort with some questions. But a pathological or practiced liar can beat the machine repeatedly. Many years ago, the U.S. Congress passed legislation banning the use of these machines in most employment settings. As the government is prone to do, it exempted itself (and certain outside contractors) from this regulation protecting employee rights. If you apply for a defense department, FBI, CIA, drug enforcement, or homeland security position, you may well be asked to take a polygraph test. Before the test, practice your deep breathing and relaxation techniques, and try to continue to use them during it. It may help your performance on the test, and, at the very least, will help reduce your stress during it.

A Mini Intelligence Test

More and more companies are turning to paper-and-pencil honesty testing despite the minor problem that *it doesn't work.* Okay, I guess it sometimes works if you actually admit that you are a lying, thieving bastard (interesting interview strategy there, eh?). But private and government studies show that thousands of honest applicants get screened out (rejected) to find the very few dishonest ones. One study showed that more than 90 percent of applicants labeled dishonest or potentially dishonest were inaccurately assessed. Boy, talk about a lawsuit waiting to happen.

This is why I suggest you view these types of tests as mini intelligence tests. First, it measures and demonstrates how uninformed (or lazy) your potential employer's hiring practices are. You need to determine if this means that there is lots of room for the improvements you can bring to this employer or whether they are so out to lunch that you want to avoid them completely.

On the other hand, this mini intelligence test applies to you, too. If you take such a test, you will see questions asking if you "ever" felt guilty or "ever" told a lie, or asking for a true-or-false to the statement that you "never" took an employer's office supplies. Be wary of questions with absolute words such as *ever* and *never*, because if you try to paint a picture of perfect sainthood, you will be labeled as attempting to fake your responses. Most of these tests are not timed, so before you start, scan it to see if you can find the repeated or very similar questions so that you respond to them consistently. Your best strategy is to review the list of positive self-descriptions you compiled to deal with the psych tests. Keep this professional, positive, but realistic image foremost in your mind and you will do fine.

Oh, and just to make you feel a little better about this stuff, drug tests, polygraph tests, and these so-called honesty tests are rarely, if ever, given to those occupying the executive suite.

YOUR FAVORITE
PROBLEM

You've worked hard, found a great opportunity, interviewed like a winner, got the job offer, negotiated it upward a bit, accepted it, and settled on a start date. Then, the unimaginable happens. You get another offer. I have seen this happen only a few times with the folks I've advised, because they usually follow my recommendation to conduct a sweep for other potential offers when they get the first one in hand. But it happens.

If the job isn't a better fit with your goals or the compensation package is far off target, your decision is easy. But if it's a better job with more compensation, your decision is tougher. Loyalty is a two-way street, and you owe an employer only the loyalty you feel you will get in return. Today's organizational reality is that if your employer's fortunes head downward, you could be gone before the next pay period. So, if you get a better job offer and you have done the analysis to *prove* it is better and you have not yet started your new job, I'd say take the better offer. If the offer is roughly equivalent, I'd say reject the new offer. If the offer is better but you've already started your new job, only take it if it is *substantially* better because, at some point, you will have to deal with the negative fallout for having "bailed out" on an employer and team that was counting on you.

It never ceases to amaze me how entire industries, professions, and multinational corporations are like small towns. Even people who don't know you personally have heard of you or they know someone who knows you. After all, that's what networking is all about. As in all areas of job hunting, be careful about burning any bridges, because, as the Little Feat song says, "The same people you misuse on your way up, you might meet 'em on the way down."

CHAPTER 9

THE WINNING JOB INTERVIEW TOOLKIT

In this chapter there are a number of tools to help you develop your winning job interview skills. There are quizzes, checklists, sample forms, typical questions, informational pieces, and practice guidelines. Some you will use only once (per job hunt) and others you will need to use time and again. Feel free to make photocopies of the ones you want to use more than once.

Most of these tools are referenced in the earlier chapters of this book. However, they are all stand-alone tools you can peruse at your convenience. There is one minor problem with these tools: They are not going to jump out of this book and go to work for you while you're snoozing on the couch. You must pull the tools out and put them to work on your behalf. Add to them; modify them; bend them to your purpose. The only mistake you can make is ignoring them.

I'd like to emphasize one more time that winning job interviewees are created, not born. It is within your power to get more and better interviews, to knock your interviewers' socks off when you get in front of them, to have glowing references, and to generate and successfully negotiate better job offers than you ever thought possible. I have shown you how to do it. All it takes from you is focus and effort. The reward of a job you love and a career that nourishes rather than diminishes you are within your grasp. Will you reach out and take it?

TOOL #1: AM I READY
TO JOB HUNT?

Directions: Answer the following questions by circling Yes or No.

1. Can I describe my job target in one or two concise sentences?   Yes   No

2. Am I willing to make my job hunt a priority by investing enough time and energy to make it successful?   Yes   No

3. Is my resume up to date?   Yes   No

4. Have I practiced my interviewing skills, preferably with videotaped role-playing?   Yes   No

5. Have I identified multiple sources of published job openings?   Yes   No

6. Have I compiled a preliminary list of my networking contacts?   Yes   No

7. Have I identified a list of appropriate employment recruiters who know my geographic target area, my functional specialty, and my industry?   Yes   No

8. Have I learned how to use the Internet to uncover job listings?   Yes   No

9. Have I asked my reference librarian what job-hunting resources are available at my local and regional libraries?   Yes   No

10. Do I know the salary range of the job for which I'm hunting?   Yes   No

11. Do I have a quiet, private place from which to make telephone calls, and voice mail to take calls when I'm not available?   Yes   No

12. Have I contacted my job references and prepared them to speak on my behalf? Yes No

13. Do I have two or three favorite interview outfits put aside in which I both look good and feel good? Yes No

14. Do I have a system set up to keep track of my job-hunting expenses so I can deduct them on my income tax return? Yes No

15. Have I discussed with my family what my new job hunt means for all of us? Yes No

Scoring:

A. If you answered yes to all 15 questions, you are well prepared to start a successful job hunt. Congratulations.

B. If you answered no to between one and three questions, you are in good shape, but you probably need to do a little more work on the foundation of your job hunt. Do it now.

C. If you answered no to more than three questions, you are not ready to start your job hunt—and you could make some critical mistakes that will hurt you in the long run. As an additional resource, find a copy of *Love Your Job! Loving the Job You Have, Finding a Job You Love* in your library or on Amazon.com, and work your way through the exercises that will get you ready to enter the job market with energy and focus.

TOOL #2: TAX TIPS
FOR THE JOB HUNTER

If you are hunting for a job in your given profession, be aware that you should be able to deduct some out-of-pocket expenses on your federal income tax return. Nothing is simple when dealing with tax returns, however, and there are ifs, buts, and maybes you need to look at. Most of all, be sure to (a) save all your receipts, and (b) consult with a CPA before taking any deductions.

If you are searching for a job in a new trade or business, your job-search expenses are not tax deductible. Naturally, "new trade or business" is not clearly defined. If a plumber becomes a lawyer, that is a new trade or business. If a taxi driver becomes a bus driver, that would not sound like a new trade or business. Under this concept, a person searching for her first job or a person after extended time out of work would not qualify for deducting his job-search expenses.

Items That Are Deductible

* Resume printing.
* Stationery and mailing of resumes and follow-up correspondence.
* Long-distance telephone calls with prospective employers.
* Internet service.
* Travel and transportation expenses for interviews or search for employment, including airfare, train fare, taxis, parking, tolls, overnight travel, meals while traveling, or automobile expenses. (Current IRS standard rate is 55¢ per mile but it changes from year to year.)
* Fees to career consultants.
* Cost of help-wanted ads and other publications.

You'll be surprised how the cost of these items can add up, so don't be shy about taking these legitimate deductions.

In order to claim these items, you must itemize your deductions. Job-search expenses fall into the miscellaneous category of deductions, which means that when combined with other miscellaneous itemized deductions, they are deductible only to the extent that they exceed 2 percent of adjusted gross income (AGI). In addition, these expenses might provide no benefit if you are subject to the alternative minimum tax (AMT). (This is why I told you to consult a CPA.)

Items That Are Not Deductible

✳ Clothing for interviews.

✳ Haircuts and other personal grooming items for interviews.

✳ Travel to locations whereby the travel is primarily personal pleasure in nature. (There goes that interview trip to Tahiti.)

I compiled this information with the invaluable assistance of John M. Hoffman & Associates, Certified Public Accountants, Chestnut Hill, Massachusetts. Any mistakes, however, are mine; so, for the third time, I'm telling you to get some professional help with your taxes.

TOOL #3: JOB HUNT GOAL-
SETTING AND MONITORING

Goals for week (or month) of _____

Obviously, you won't be engaging in every one of these job-search activities every week. Tailor your goals to the appropriate stage of your job hunt. Don't gloss over this tool. Setting clear goals and honestly measuring your progress toward them will help you refine and customize your plan with up-to-the-minute results and feedback.

Part I

My current job targets(s):

	Projected	Actual
1. Hours to invest in job hunt.	____	____
2. Hours to find and respond to published openings.	____	____
3. Hours to research potential employers and do targeted mailing.	____	____

	Projected	Actual
4. Hours to identify and contact agencies, recruiters, and search consultants.		
5. Hours to read job-hunting books.		
6. Hours to scan job-listing Websites.		
7. Hours to identify, contact, and expand personal network (total):		
a. By phone.		
b. By e-mail.		
c. In person.		
8. Hours to identify and prepare job references.		
9. Hours to practice interviewing skills.		
10. Hours in actual interviews.		
11. Hours for administrative activities (filing, copying, thank-you letters).		
12. Other.		
13. Other.		

Part II

Based on the evaluation in Part I:

1. What's working:_____

_____

2. What's not working: _____

_____

3. I need to increase:_____

_____

4. I need to decrease:_____

_____

5. Other feedback/changes I should make: _____

_____

6. My reward for accomplishing these goals: _____

_____

TOOL #4: RESEARCH
RESOURCES

After a few weeks of active job hunting, it is going to be hard for you to remember all the sources of useful information you uncovered, where you found them, who helped you find them, and where they are physically located. Whenever you find a helpful research resource, log in the relevant data. You may have to quickly find this information again as you prepare for upcoming interviews, during job-offer analysis and negotiation, or future job searches.

Helpful data:_____

Source of data: _____

How to find data: _____

Date found: _____

Library or database:_____

Physical location: _____

Name of reference librarian or contact: _____

Helpful data:_____

Source of data: _____

How to find data:_____

Date found: _____

Library or database:_____

Physical location:_____

Name of reference librarian or contact: _____

Helpful data:_____

Source of data: _____

How to find data: _____

Date found: _____

Library or database:_____

Physical location: _____

Name of reference librarian or contact: _____

TOOL #5: BUILDING YOUR
CONTACT NETWORK

I. How you build, maintain, utilize, and grow your network of personal contacts will have an overarching effect on your ability to generate job leads and interviews. A few facts:

1. Your contact network will only expand from this moment forward.

2. It would be fantastic if any of your contacts has a bona fide job opening for you, but this is unlikely. Your goal is to gather two things from your contacts: (1) data you can use to generate job leads, and (2) access to new contacts. (See Section II.)

3. Your initial network of contacts is larger than you think. (See Section III.)

4. You will get more usable information from those farthest away from your initial list of contacts. (Remember the strength of weak ties.) Thus, the very essence of effective networking is *expanding* your network.

5. There is no rule that says you can ask a contact for ideas and leads only once during your job search. Every couple of weeks you can "keep them posted" on your progress and tap them for new input.

II. Don't beat around the bush. Tell everyone on your initial contact list that you are starting a job search and hope you can count on their help. Assuming they say yes, tell them what you are looking for and ask the following questions:

1. Do they know of any immediate openings of the sort you are looking for? Do they have a contact name for you? Can they make an introduction?

2. What sources of published openings are they familiar with (places to find job postings, help-wanted ads, newspapers, Websites, job banks, alumni groups, association or professional newsletters, and so on)?

3. What libraries, research resources, or databases have they found helpful in their job searches?

4. What is their sense of your industry/company targets? Do they have any inside sources?

5. Do they know any employment agencies, contingency recruiters, or executive search consultants to whom they can introduce you?

6. Will they give you the names and numbers of four or five folks they know whom they think have the best or widest network you might be able to tap into to find more of this same type of information?

Close the conversation with your thanks and let them know you'll periodically be "keeping them posted." (See Section I, Question 5.)

III. The key to thoroughly identifying your initial contact list is to ask yourself what constituencies you are a member of. The more extensive your initial contact list is, the more extensive your expanded contact network list will be, the more job leads you will generate, the more interviews you will land, the more offers you will get, and, ultimately, the shorter your job search will be. To help you build this critical first level of network contacts, list the people you know who are members of the following groups.

1. Your family (immediate and extended).

2. Your in-laws (current and former).

3. Your friends and social group.

4. Your current work colleagues/acquaintance group (discretion is advised).

5. Your current customers, vendors, suppliers, and consultants.

6. Your colleagues from previous jobs.

7. Your bosses from previous jobs.

8. Customers, vendors, suppliers, and consultants from previous jobs.

9. People you've met at professional meetings, conferences, and conventions.

10. People in your technical, professional, or trade groups.

11. Your job references.

12. People with whom you have interviewed in the past.

13. Neighbors and former neighbors.

14. Personal contacts from school (yours and spouse's).

15. People you've met in the PTA.

16. Your holiday card list.

17. Members of your church, social, civic, athletic, community, and political groups.

18. Your alumni association.

19. Your personal consultants (for example, attorney, clergy, accountant, hairdresser, mechanic, dentist, insurance person).

20. Contacts from any job-search groups you join.

I've combined a number of these groups together, but you catch my drift. You know more people than you think you do. Now go to work and turn them into a network that can help you land a job you love.

TOOL #6: FREQUENTLY ASKED INTERVIEW QUESTIONS

As you prepare for your interviews, read each question and prepare a solid answer for it. You may not get the exact same questions in your interview, but you will probably get some that are quite close.

As you have read in Chapter 4, I want you to practice your interviewing skills in hour-long, videotaped mock interviews. Before you start this process, identify the questions you want your interviewer to use, but allow him to choose some to throw in as well.

A. Your personal qualities
1. What are your greatest strengths?
2. What are your greatest weaknesses?
3. How would your colleagues describe you?
4. What types of people rub you the wrong way?
5. How do you handle conflict?
6. Tell me about yourself.
7. What is unique about you?
8. What turns you off?
9. Are you a born leader or a natural follower?
10. What motivates you?
11. Are you a better written communicator or a better verbal communicator?
12. Tell me how you handled a difficult social situation.
13. What are your hobbies and interests? What do you do in your spare time?
14. What is your energy level like?
15. How have you learned from your disappointments?
16. Do you prefer working with others or working alone?
17. Describe your personality.
18. What bores you? Why? How do you avoid it?
19. What public figure do you admire? Why?
20. What do you want out of life?

B. Your education
1. How did you do in high school? Favorite and worst courses, teachers? Sports, activities, offices held?
2. Why did you choose the college you attended?
3. Why did you choose your course of study?
4. Did you enjoy school? Why/why not?

5. What extracurricular activities were you involved in? Were they worth the time you put into them?

6. How much of your schooling did you pay for yourself? How?

7. Did you work while you were in school? Doing what? Did it help or hurt your grades?

8. How did your academic/training background prepare you for this job/organization?

9. If you could do your schooling over, what would you change? Why?

10. Could you have done better in school? How? Why didn't you?

11. What continuing professional training have you completed since graduating?

12. What are your future educational plans? What have you done about them?

C. Your career

1. Explain your career path to me.

2. What was your first job? What did you learn from it? (Same question for every other job.)

3. Who was your favorite boss? Why?

4. Who was your worst boss? Why?

5. What parts of your schoolwork most prepared you for work? How?

6. What obstacles have you had to overcome to succeed?

7. Where do you see yourself in three, five, and 10 years?

8. Explain how you operate in a team environment.

9. Should people in your field be paid more?

10. What are your financial goals? Are you on track to reach them?

11. What is the difference in the way you treat subordinates versus superiors?

12. How have you handled a disagreement with a boss? With a peer?
13. Have you ever been fired? Why?
14. Have you ever fired someone? How?
15. From your resume, show me a good example of teamwork.
16. From your resume, show me a good example of your work ethic and initiative.
17. Have you had any jobs that do not appear on your resume?
18. What are your greatest accomplishments?
19. Tell me about a big mistake that you made at work.
20. What types of people will you not work with?
21. How long do you want to continue working?
22. What are the disadvantages of your chosen field?
23. Do you prefer a large or small company?
24. Will you go where the company sends you?
25. Looking back over your career, what do you wish you had done differently?
26. Where do you see your career going?

D. This job
1. How did you hear about this opening?
2. Why should we hire you for this job?
3. What do you bring to this job that is different from anyone else?
4. Why do you want to leave your current job/company?
5. How much are you currently making? How much do you want to make?
6. What are you looking for in your next job?
7. Evaluate your current boss for me.
8. What do you like best about your current job?

9. Why did you receive your last promotion?

10. How does this job compare with others you've applied for?

11. What are some things you and your boss have disagreed about?

12. What is it about this job that appeals to you most?

13. In what ways has your current job prepared you for this one?

14. How does this job fit in with your overall career plans?

15. What makes you think you can succeed in this job?

16. What are your short-term objectives?

17. What other organizations are you interviewing with?

18. What aspect of this job excites you the most?

19. How would you modify this position to best suit your skills?

20. Can I check your references?

21. When can you start?

22. If we offer you this job, will you accept it?

23. Will you stay with your current employer if they make you a counteroffer?

24. What is your transition plan for the job you're leaving?

25. What will your current boss say/do when you tell her you're leaving?

E. This company

1. What do you know about our company?

2. What attracts you to our organization?

3. What is our reputation in the marketplace?

4. What have you learned about our organizational culture?

5. Why do you think this company will be any better than your last?

6. Whom do you know who works for us?

7. How familiar are you with our products or services?

8. What do you specifically bring to our company that it needs?

9. Have you read our annual report?

10. What research have you done about our organization?

11. Have you read any articles about us in the press?

12. Can you see spending the rest of your career with us?

F. General

1. What's most important to you?

2. Are you interested in sports? The arts?

3. Do you do charity work? Are you involved in your community?

4. What did your parents do for work? Which one has had the biggest influence on you?

5. Do you have brothers or sisters?

6. What was your military service?

7. Who are your best friends?

8. What great selling point about you haven't I yet learned?

9. How are you planning for your retirement?

10. Are you nervous?

11. Will you take a drug test as a condition of employment?

12. Do you have any questions?

TOOL #7: PREPARING WINNING
INTERVIEW QUESTIONS TO ASK

1. The job for which you are interviewing: ————————

2. The person with whom you're interviewing: ————————

3. List key facts you have learned about:

    a. The industry: ————————————————

    b. The organization: ————————————————

    c. The job itself: ————————————————

    d. Your interviewer: ————————————————

4. Which elements of your background (school, previous jobs, special knowledge or skills) do you think might be particularly attractive to this employer?

    ————————————————————————————————

5. Which of your personal characteristics or qualities do you want to highlight in this interview?

    ————————————————————————————————

6. What data do you need from inside the organization to help you decide if you would accept a job offer from them?

    ————————————————————————————————

Based upon all of the data here, carefully construct four winning questions to ask in this interview.

1. ————————————————————————————————

————————————————————————————————

2. ————————————————————————————————

————————————————————————————————

3. ————————————————————————————————

————————————————————————————————

4. ————————————————————————————————

————————————————————————————————

TOOL #8: MOCK INTERVIEW
PREPARATION TOOL

1. Interviewer; location of interview: _____

2. Video camera ready and tested? _____

3. Resume on hand? _____

4. What is this job? _____

5. Why is it open? _____

6. Background of organization: _____
   _____

7. List of questions candidate wants to practice (10 to 12):
   _____
   _____
   _____
   _____
   _____
   _____
   _____
   _____
   _____
   _____

8. List of questions interviewer wants to add in (6 to 8):
   _____
   _____
   _____
   _____
   _____
   _____
   _____

9. Start time: _____

10. Finish time: _____

TOOL #9: MOCK INTERVIEW
EVALUATION TOOL

1. Opening:
   a. Handshake.
   b. Facial expression/body language.
   c. Was generally strong or weak.
   d. Ideas for improvement.
2. How tense or stressed was the candidate?
3. Any distracting verbal habits?
4. Any distracting physical habits?
5. What questions were handled well?
6. What questions need work? How?
7. Did the candidate try to uncover any potential objections? How did it come across?
8. Did the candidate succeed at overturning any potential objections? Ideas for improvement?
9. Did the candidate use a strong close? How could it have been improved?
10. How else could this candidate have improved this interview?

TOOL #10: JOB INTERVIEW
PREPARATION TOOL

1. Have I prepared for this interview (research and practice)?
2. Where and when is it?
3. Interviewer (any background)?
4. What is this job?
5. Why is it open?

6. Background of organization?

7. Copies of resume and references on hand?

8. My selling points regarding this position:

9. Well-prepared questions I want to ask:

   a. _____

   b. _____

   c. _____

10. Trial closes I've practiced:

    a. _____

    b. _____

    c. _____

11. Possible objections I've prepared for:

    a. Potential objection: _____

        Need clarifying question? _____

        Response to overturn or address: _____

        Strong point to end on: _____

    b. Potential objection: _____

        Need clarifying question? _____

        Response to overturn or address: _____

        Strong point to end on: _____

    c. Potential objection: _____

        Need clarifying question? _____

        Response to overturn or address: _____

        Strong point to end on: _____

12. Here's how I'll ask for the job: _____

TOOL #11: JOB REFERENCE
DATA FORM

Today's date: _____

Name and current title: _____

Mailing address:_____

Date of first thank-you note: _____

Date(s) of subsequent thank-you notes: _____

_____

E-mail address: _____

Preferred telephone number: _____

Best way and time to reach: _____

Known for how long: _____

From when and where: _____

Reference's job then: _____

My job then: _____

My strengths: _____

My weaknesses: _____

My personality: _____

My supervisory/management style: _____

_____

Why I left: _____

_____

Would I be rehired: _____

Fit with new position: _____

Career goals: _____

_____

_____

List other appropriate questions from Chapter 5.

TOOL #12: SAMPLE JOB
REFERENCE LISTING SHEET

You may be asked for your job references in person, over the phone, or by e-mail. You may be asked to actually supply a written list (like the sample following), or you may be able to give them verbally. Either way, you should have a neat, updated, accurate reference listing sheet ready to offer or to read from.

Job References
for
Ms. Ivanna Tankul

Richard W. Smith
Vice President, Land Development
Lincolnville Savings & Loan
phone: (123) 456-7890
former boss

Edward Deevy
Eire Investments LLC
phone: (123) 456-7890
former boss (from Coastal Mutual Insurance)

Gail Gentile
President
Persuasive Credit and Collections, Inc.
phone: (123) 456-7890
work closely with Ms. Gentile (an outside vendor) in my current job

Jeffery A. Harrison
Owner
Berkshire Blasting & Drilling
phone: (123) 456-7890
former boss from part-time college job

TOOL #13: POST-INTERVIEW
EVALUATION AND IMPROVEMENT TOOL

1. Date, time, location of interview; interviewer's name, title:
2. The job:
3. Was my research on target?
4. What new information did I learn about the job? The employer?
5. What question was I unprepared for?
6. What question did I stumble on?
7. What answers did the interviewer love?
8. What were the best questions I asked?
9. What questions do I wish I had asked?
10. What trial close did I use?
11. What objections did I uncover?
12. How did my "overturn/address" responses work?
13. How did I handle the issue of money?
14. Did I clearly state that I wanted the job?
15. Did I get a sense of the hiring process timeline?
16. Did I smile, keep eye contact, and use a firm handshake?
17. Did I learn something personal about the interviewer?
18. Do I have a follow-up thank-you letter ready to go?
19. What further research do I need to do before my next interview?
20. How would I grade this interview performance?

TOOL #14: JOB OFFER
ANALYSIS TOOL

You should be able to answer all of the following questions before you decide if a job is right for you. Some of these questions can also guide you in your preinterview research and can help you to design useful questions to ask in the interview itself.

1. The job as offered:
2. How does it fit with current job target(s)?
3. Is it a unique or unusual opportunity?
4. Scope of responsibility:
5. Move ahead, lateral, or down?
6. Biggest selling point:
7. Biggest drawback:
8. Assess prospective boss:
9. Assess prospective colleagues:
10. Assess prospective subordinates:
11. Others in organization I want to work with:
12. Organization's future prospects (for example, merger, buyout, consolidation, sale):
13. Assess organization's reputation:
14. Assess organization's culture:
15. Opportunity for promotion:
16. Internal training/development program(s):
17. Opportunity for outside visibility:
18. Lifestyle/family issues (for example, travel, relocation, nights, weekends, overtime):
19. Who else has data I can access:
20. My gut says:
21. Issues for me to negotiate:

TOOL# 15: COMPENSATION
PACKAGE EVALUATION TOOL

	Minimum	Current Target	Current Offer
Base salary			
Signing bonus			
Yearly bonus			
Moving or relocation costs			
Incentive plan			
Profit sharing			
Deferred compensation plan			
401(k), other matching program, or stock plan			
Pension or other retirement vehicle			
Sales quota, commissions, overrides, etc.			
Expense account			
Vacation			
Holidays, sick days, personal days			
Employment contract or guaranteed outplacement			

	Minimum	Current Target	Current Offer
Medical insurance (individual or family plan?)			
Dental insurance (individual or family plan?)			
Life insurance			
Short-/long-term disability insurance			
Company car or car allowance			
Daycare/eldercare			
Parking			
Association memberships			
Club memberships			
Other			

TOOL #16: JOB SEARCH
WRAP-UP TOOL

Directions: Respond to the following items by circling Yes or No. By taking appropriate action, convert every no to a yes before you start your new assignment.

1. I have accepted my job offer verbally and in writing.   Yes   No

2. I have a firm start date.   Yes   No

3. I have sent personalized thank-you/ announcement letters to all the librarians and research assistants who helped me during this job hunt.   Yes   No

4. I have sent personalized thank-you/
   announcement letters to all the agencies,
   recruiters, and search consultants I contacted
   during this search.   Yes   No

5. I have sent personalized thank-you/
   announcement letters to everyone who actually
   interviewed me during this job hunt.   Yes   No

6. I have sent personalized thank-you/
   announcement letters to all my job references.   Yes   No

7. I have sent a thank-you/announcement letter to
   every person in my new and expanded contact
   network.   Yes   No

8. I have captured all of my relevant job-search
   expense receipts for use in my next tax return.   Yes   No

9. I have completed the Research Resources Tool
   (#4) so I can get my next job search up to
   speed more quickly.   Yes   No

10. I have kept copies of all the letters I found
    useful during my job hunt.   Yes   No

11. I have committed to respond to every
    headhunter call I get in the future to build my
    contacts in this area.   Yes   No

12. I will take some definite action to ensure that
    my contact network continues to expand.   Yes   No

13. I have committed to network with any job
    hunter who appropriately asks for my input or
    assistance.   Yes   No

14. I have explicitly thanked my family for
    supporting me (okay, putting up with me)
    during this job search.   Yes   No

15. I have something planned to celebrate this
    significant achievement.   Yes   No

ONWARD

AND UPWARD

Typically, this section would be called a conclusion or a summary, or maybe even an epilogue. But you may be one of those readers who thumbs back and forth through a book before really digging into the material to find what you need most at that moment in time. Or maybe you have already started to put yourself out there actively in the job market and are just starting to get some solid interview practice under your belt. Perhaps you are well into a second or third round of interviews and are now concentrating on negotiating the best deal possible. I'd love it if you have just landed a great job but wisely realize that this is not *really* an end, only a new beginning. In any event, there is no "concluding" this process, only moving forward—onward and upward to the next challenge.

I can't help that uncertainty, rejection, and anxiety are all part and parcel of the job-hunting process. But so are discovery, enthusiasm, and acceptance. If you allow yourself to focus on the potential negatives, stress and anxiety will creep into your interviews like a fog. Thus, you must train yourself to focus on the eventual positives, and that fog will evaporate before your very eyes in the warmth of your realistic optimism.

I've tried to pack this book with tons of information, and as many shortcuts as I can think of, and I've tried to boil everything down to its bare bones so that you start to see some results fast. I've coached you, I've counseled you, and I've given you the best advice I have to get you moving in the right direction. I've laid in some humor to keep you smiling while you suffer the slings and arrows of outrageous fortune. (Surprise, surprise—you didn't think I was going to go literary on you at the last minute, did you?) What I can't do, however, is go out there and do it for you. I wish I could, because, if we met, and after I spent some time getting to know you, I could convince almost any employer why they should hire you, and no one else but you. Because I would dig that information out of its truest source: you.

So we end up back where we started: asking the big questions. What are you looking for; why; what knowledge, skills, and experience do you bring to the table; what is it about you—your unique blend of personal qualities and characteristics—that will ensure your success in this new job?

A couple of folks with whom I've worked throughout the years have fantasized about us using one of those miniature radio devices so I could listen in on their interviews and then whisper great responses into their ears for them to use. Let this book act as that device for you. If you go through it from cover to cover you will hear me prodding you to always outprepare your competition. You will hear me joking with you to help you get your anxiety under control and working for, not against you. You will hear me reassure you that you have a fail-safe answer for anything they throw at you. You will hear me tell you—even if no one else ever has—that you deserve a job you love and that it is out there if only you'll do the work to go out and find it.

I wish you strength, courage, and humor on this voyage, and until our paths cross again may God hold you in the palm of His hand.

INDEX

J

K

L

M

ABOUT THE

AUTHOR

Dr. Paul Powers has devoted 30 years to helping others achieve career success and satisfaction. As a management psychologist, executive coach, author, and career expert, he has helped thousands of people in hundreds of companies—from CEOs to recent grads, from corporations, hospitals, and recent combat veterans—to find and succeed in jobs they love. He advises corporations worldwide on how to select, motivate, and lead fully engaged employees with executive coaching, management and sales team development, and pre-retirement planning.

As a popular speaker and seminar leader, Dr. Paul travels extensively, sharing his wisdom, his humor, and his deepest belief that each of us has a gift to be discovered, developed, and shared. As author of *Winning Job Interviews* and coauthor of *Love Your Job! Loving the Job You Have, Finding a Job You Love*, Paul's energy, enthusiasm, and motivation have reached around the world to people in every imaginable field.

Dr. Powers is a licensed psychologist, the former chairman of the Massachusetts Board of Psychologists, and a member of numerous professional organizations. Paul holds a bachelor's, master's, and doctoral degree in psychology from the University of Massachusetts at

Amherst. He helped found the Management Corps for the Emerging East, a nonprofit initiative to send American business volunteers to work in enterprises of the republics of the former Soviet Union to assist in their transition to a free market economy with hands-on management skills and techniques. Paul is also a former U.S. Marine as well as a former licensed pipe fitter.

Dr. Powers's work has been widely noted in the media such as the *Wall Street Journal*, *New York Times*, *National Business Employment Weekly*, *New England Business Magazine*, and hundreds of newspapers and radio stations nationwide, and he has appeared on CNN, MSNBC, WNBC, NPR, and numerous other media outlets. He cohosted *CareerTalk*, a call-in show on a major Boston radio station.

Practicing what he preaches about the many benefits of developing varied interests, Paul also maintains a specialized forensic practice, is a voice-over artist, is an avid outdoorsman, and has an active pro bono schedule nationally and internationally. He divides his time between Massachusetts and Florida with his wife, Linda, who is an entrepreneur, graphic designer, and principal of Powers Design.

Tired of boring meetings? Have Dr. Paul speak at your organization's next off-site meeting, conference, or association event with a fast-moving, practical, and engaging presentation from an acknowledged leader in the field of career and personal success. E-mail him at drpaul@drpaulpowers.com. Sign up for a free subscription to his LifeMap newsletter, read by thousands, at *www.drpaulpowers.com*.